MW00399723

The
KIND OF
PREACHING
GOD
BLESSES

STEVEN J. LAWSON

HARVEST HOUSE PUBLISHERS
EUGENE, OREGON

Cover by Dugan Design Group, Bloomington, Minnesota

Published in association with the literary agency of Wolgemuth & Associates, Inc.

THE KIND OF PREACHING GOD BLESSES
Copyright © 2013 by Steven J. Lawson
Published by Harvest House Publishers
Eugene, Oregon 97402
www.harvesthousepublishers.com

ISBN 978-0-7369-5355-9 (pbk.)
ISBN 978-0-7369-5356-6 (eBook)

Printed in China

13 14 15 16 17 18 19 20 21 / RDS-KBD / 10 9 8 7 6 5 4 3 2 1

*This book is dedicated to
my brother-in-law,
who has been a major source of encouragement
to me for over three decades—*

Drew Crowell

*whose life has been
a strong witness for the Lord Jesus Christ
and whose love of the Scriptures
and the spiritual well-being of others
has been mightily used for the kingdom of God.*

Contents

When I came to you, brethren, I did not come with superiority of speech or of wisdom, proclaiming to you the testimony of God. For I determined to know nothing among you except Jesus Christ, and Him crucified. I was with you in weakness and in fear and in much trembling, and my message and my preaching were not in persuasive words of wisdom, but in demonstration of the Spirit and of power, so that your faith would not rest on the wisdom of men, but on the power of God. Yet we do speak wisdom among those who are mature; a wisdom, however, not of this age nor of the rulers of this age, who are passing away; but we speak God's wisdom in a mystery, the hidden wisdom which God predestined before the ages to our glory; the wisdom which none of the rulers of this age has understood; for if they had understood it they would not have crucified the Lord of glory; but just as it is written, "Things which eye has not seen and ear has not heard, and which have not entered the heart of man, all that God has prepared for those who love Him."

—1 Corinthians 2:1-9

Foreword
The Kind of Preaching God Blesses

John MacArthur

For the faithful preacher, 2 Timothy 4:2 majestically stands out as sacred ground. It is precious territory for every pastor who, following in the footsteps of Paul, desires to faithfully proclaim the Word of God. In this single verse, the apostle defined the primary mandate for God-honoring church ministry, not only for Timothy, but for all who would come after him. The minister of the gospel is called to "preach the word."

The faithful expositor understands that Scripture is no ordinary book. The power of the pulpit is in the Word preached, as the Spirit uses His sword to pierce human hearts (Ephesians 6:17; Hebrews 4:12). This sacred book is "inspired by God," or more literally, God-breathed. It is not only powerful to save, but also to sanctify. Consequently, the pastor's task is to faithfully feed the flock with the pure milk of the Word (1 Peter 2:1-3), trusting God for the resulting growth.

With such a comprehensive work of both salvation and sanctification available through the power of the Scriptures, why would anyone be tempted to preach anything else? The pastor who cares about the spiritual growth of his people must make God and His Word the centerpiece of his ministry. In order to do that, he must preach the Word.

God is still delivering His divine mandate to faithful men to preach the Word, and this sacred charge certainly compels Steven Lawson, who powerfully and passionately demonstrates his obedience to this divine commission. A proven example to this and future generations of preachers, he offers in this book a clarion call to the kind of preaching God blesses.

Lawson is passionate about biblical preaching. He understands that careful biblical exposition from the pulpit is the great need of the church today. His own preaching ministry is exemplary. As a faithful preacher for many years, he has been widely appreciated for the boldness, clarity, and care with which he handles Scripture.

In this present hour, Lawson says that a dearth of biblical preaching has left the evangelical movement weak, starving for spiritual truth, and susceptible to the ravages of the enemy. I am convinced he is right.

With great precision, like that of a skilled surgeon, Lawson cuts directly to the heart issue of preaching in this generation. With pinpoint accuracy, he gives the correct diagnosis to the pulpit ailment that plagues so many churches in this day. Lawson rightly concludes that there is certainly no shortage of preaching. Rather, the problem lies in the anemic substance and lack of power in the evangelical pulpit.

Far too often, today's messages contain everything except the main thing. They are devoid of the preaching of Christ in all His glory. Therefore, pulpits are powerless to save.

Tragically, this kind of empty preaching has gone viral, reaching pandemic levels throughout churches across this globe. The evidence seems overwhelming. Preaching itself is on the decline in a major way. Numerous churches—including some of the largest and best-known ones—have relegated the pulpit ministry to second-class status.

To this end, Lawson states the much-needed cure. If there is to be a reformation of the pulpit, and a revival again in the church, it will only come about through God-glorifying, Christ-centered, Spirit-empowered preaching. This and this alone is the kind of preaching God blesses—*biblical* preaching.

Here is a wonderful antidote for preachers confused by all the modern emphasis on style over substance. Lawson takes us back to the Scriptures, specifically 1 Corinthians 2:1-9, to show how *biblical* preaching is mandated by God and exemplified by the apostle Paul. It is both challenging and encouraging.

I am very thankful to see this book in print, and I pray

that it will have a widespread impact on pastors, church leaders, young preachers-to-be, and the famished members of our flocks.

May this work be a sword in the Holy Spirit's arsenal to equip and embolden many steadfast men to such noble faithfulness and promised blessing.

John MacArthur
Pastor/Teacher
Grace Community Church
Sun Valley, California

Preface
The Greatest Need
of the Hour

The Priority of Biblical Preaching

Not all sermons are the same. Some messages rise above others in the impact and influence they exert. Such a word brings the right emphasis, for the right group, at the right time. It is a timely word that uniquely addresses a pressing need for an appointed hour. This kind of divinely appointed message arises out of the deep conviction of the preacher and connects with the heart of the hearer.

To be sure, this message succeeds because God causes it to triumph. The wind blows, Jesus says, wherever and whenever it wishes. Even so, the Holy Spirit moves sovereignly and irresistibly upon the lives of people as the Word is preached. By His supreme authority, God causes a particular message to fulfill its intended purpose.

This was definitely the case with a sermon I recently delivered in different places around the world. It was a message strategically fit for the moment—a sermon unusually blessed by God. In expanded form, these addresses comprise the essential content of this book.

HOW IT ALL BEGAN

Moody Bible Institute's Pastors' Conference

On Tuesday morning, May 24, 2011, I flew to Chicago, Illinois, to speak at the annual Pastors' Conference at Moody Bible Institute. With a sizable group of pastors and Christian workers in attendance in Torrey-Gray Auditorium, I delivered an exposition of 1 Corinthians 2:1-9 titled "The Kind of Preaching God Blesses."

At that time, I was preaching verse-by-verse through the book of 1 Corinthians at Christ Fellowship Baptist Church in Mobile, Alabama. Remembering how God had empowered my messages from these verses, I compressed my notes into one sermon for this special occasion. With a few revisions, I took this manuscript to Chicago for this strategic conference.

What happened that day at Moody Bible Institute far exceeded my expectations. As I stepped into the pulpit, the Holy Spirit quickened my mind, bringing to my remembrance what I had written in my notes. As I spoke, the Spirit deepened my convictions, increasing my confidence in the truths in the passage. Further, He impassioned my heart, enflaming my passions with zeal. The pastors, I discerned, were particularly attentive to the Word being preached. It was clear from their positive response that the Lord had struck a live nerve with these men that day.

Samara, Russia

Upon leaving Chicago, I immediately flew to the other side of the world, to Samara, Russia, where I was to preach at the graduation service for the Samara Center for Biblical Training. Earlier, I had asked the leadership of the school what would be the most appropriate message for this gathering. After laying out several options, the overwhelming response was that I should preach the same message I had just delivered in Chicago from 1 Corinthians 2:1-9, namely "The Kind of Preaching God Blesses."

Speaking through an interpreter, I once again declared what Paul identified as "the testimony of God." I brought this same message not to simplify the demands of my preaching schedule, but because I discerned that these same truths must be heralded to this group of Russian pastors. In addressing these graduates, the sermon struck the same note, that not all preaching is the same. There is a kind of preaching that God blesses, specifically the proclamation that exalts the crucified Christ by the power of the Spirit. Conversely, there is a kind of preaching that God does not bless, a mere echoing of man's empty wisdom that is devoid of Christ.

With many man-centered influences in ministry being imported into the former Soviet Union, this message was timely for the Russian church. Those pastors desperately needed to hear this truth trumpeted in their ears. In light of the raging pragmatism invading the Russian church, these men direly needed to have this message resonate in their hearts. They needed to be reminded, as we all do, that apart from Christ and Him crucified, the preacher has nothing to say. These pastors needed to hear that it is the divine message, not gospel gimmicks, that should singularly mark their preaching ministries.

Shepherds' Conference

Almost one year later, on March 9, 2012, I had the privilege of preaching at the Shepherds' Conference at Grace Community Church in Sun Valley, California, hosted by John MacArthur. Assembled for this occasion was a large, international contingency of pastors and missionaries from all 50 states and 48 nations around the globe. There is not another gathering of strong men like this conference anywhere in the world.

As I considered what I should preach, I was reminded how God had blessed the preaching of His Word from 1 Corinthians 2:1-9—first in Mobile, then Chicago, and finally, Samara. Sensing His divine leading, I reworked my notes from these prior occasions and took them into the pulpit to deliver this same message, "The Kind of Preaching God Blesses." Again, God empowered me in the proclamation of this passage, though with a strength certainly not my own. I seemed to be a mere observer of my own sermon. Afterward, I was to meet with a Christian publisher and his editor to discuss a possible writing project. As we sat down in a borrowed office at Grace Church, I was emotionally spent from having just preached this message.

In fact, I personally felt as though I was woefully inadequate in my presentation. I had not delivered the message as I had anticipated, and felt that I had failed in my assignment as a herald of divine truth.

As I met with this publishing team, I apologized for my feeble efforts in the pulpit. But before I could finish my words, the publisher abruptly said, "I would like to publish this message as a book. I believe every minister needs to hear this sermon." Needless to say, I was stunned.

At that very moment, John MacArthur walked into this small office. To my amazement, he was looking for me. He approached me and, likewise, affirmed the same, saying, "That was exactly what we needed to hear." I was speechless.

Astonished that God would use me in spite of my enormous weakness, I realized that this particular message had put its finger upon a live nerve in the body of Christ. Far beyond my control, all I could do was ride this wave of providence, going wherever it took me.

Ligonier National Conference

In God's perfect timing, I was to preach the following week, on March 17, at Ligonier Ministries' 2012 National Conference in Orlando, Florida, with R.C. Sproul. The theme of this conference was "The Christian Mind," and months earlier, the Ligonier team had assigned me to preach "Foolishness to the Greeks." In this message, I was asked to address how unintelligible the gospel is to the unregenerate mind.

Given this specific assignment, I felt I had no option but to preach this same text. For a fifth time, I expounded this very same passage in 1 Corinthians. Only this time, I addressed the larger context of 1 Corinthians 1:18–2:5. As I preached this passage, the Spirit again carried me along, as though borne on wings of eagles.

On each occasion, from Mobile to Chicago, Samara, Los Angeles, and Orlando, God unusually blessed the preaching of His Word. This book that you now hold is an integrated record of what I delivered during these five preaching assignments, along with some further expansions. As you read this book, I pray that the blessing of God may accompany these same truths as they go forward in the power of His Spirit.

AS THE PULPIT GOES

God knows how desperately preachers today must return to what is set forth in this signature text about preaching. As the pulpit goes, so goes the church. Never has this been more true than it is in this present hour. The fact remains, no church can rise any higher than its pulpit. The spiritual life of any congregation and its growth in grace will never exceed the high-water mark set by its pulpit.

This book goes forth with a prayer that the Sovereign Head of the church, the Lord Jesus Christ, will raise up a new generation of God-exalting, Christ-centered, Spirit-energized preachers. May they be faithful, fervent proclaimers of Christ and Him crucified, who preach in the power of the Holy Spirit. Such preaching remains the most urgent need in this present hour.

AN EXPRESSION OF THANKS

Before we begin, I want to thank the publishing team at Harvest House, who heard this message preached at the Shepherds' Conference and initiated having its truths put into print. I am grateful for Bob Hawkins, the publisher, and Steve Miller, my editor, for their vision for this project.

I must thank Christ Fellowship Baptist Church of Mobile, Alabama, whom I have the privilege and pleasure of serving as senior pastor. They have eagerly received my preaching of 1 Corinthians, which is, admittedly, not an easy book under which to sit. This Pauline epistle is, in reality, a spiritual spanking in response to what was occurring in the church at Corinth, though it leads to great blessing. The material in this book originates from this expository series at Christ Fellowship.

I am also grateful for the support of my fellow elders at CFBC, who encourage me in my extended ministry abroad. I especially want to express my gratitude to my executive assistant, Kay Allen, who typed this entire document, and Keith Phillips, a fellow pastor at Christ Fellowship, who helped in the preparation of this manuscript.

Finally, I must acknowledge my family for providing me with much encouragement in my personal life and preaching ministry. My wife, Anne, and our four children, Andrew, James, Grace Anne, and John, stand with me in their support.

Soli Deo gloria,
Steven J. Lawson
Christ Fellowship Baptist Church
Mobile, Alabama
July 2012

1
Everything Except
the Main Thing

The Poverty of Modern Preaching

There is no shortage of preaching in the world today. The sheer number of churches across the globe bears evidence of this very fact. In many places, there is a church building on every corner and within every church, a pulpit, and in every pulpit, preaching.

But the reality is that not all preaching is the same. There is the kind of preaching that God blesses, and there is that which He abandons. There is the kind of preaching that has the favor of heaven upon it, and there is that which is a mere exercise in empty rhetoric. There is a world of difference between the two.

What so desperately needs to be recovered in this present hour is not merely more preaching. Instead, what is urgently required is more preaching of a certain kind. The problem today is not the scarcity of preaching. No, the issue lies with the utter bankruptcy of so much that passes for preaching today.

By any spiritual estimation, something is horribly missing in the contemporary pulpit. This dearth in preaching is nothing short of a modern-day famine for the hearing of the words of the Lord. We live in a time of severe drought for the proclamation of Jesus Christ and Him crucified that is Spirit-empowered. There are few clouds in sight, and no rain is forecast. Sadly, there is enough dust on the average pulpit Bible to write *Ichabod* upon it.

A MOST DIABOLICAL STRATEGY

Years ago, Donald Grey Barnhouse, pastor of Tenth Presbyterian Church in Philadelphia, Pennsylvania, delivered a message that aired on CBS radio. In this nationwide address, the noted Bible teacher speculated about what would be the most diabolical strategy that Satan could conspire against the church in the years to come.

To the astonishment of many listeners, Barnhouse imagined that all of the bars in Philadelphia would be closed. Prostitutes would no longer walk the streets. Pornography would no longer be available. The streets would be clean, and all the city neighborhoods would be filled with law-abiding citizens. All swearing and cursing would be gone. Children would respectfully say, "Yes, sir" and "No, ma'am."

Every church in town, Barnhouse added, would be packed to overflowing. There would not be one church pew that could contain one more citizen.

What, you ask, could be wrong with this?

Barnhouse then delivered the knockout punch. The deadliest, most diabolical danger, he said, would be that in each of these filled-to-capacity sanctuaries, Jesus Christ would *never* be preached.

In these pulpits, there would be much religious talk, but nothing said of the supreme authority and saving work of Christ upon the cross. There would be mention of morality, but no Christ. There would be expressions of cultural concern and political commentary, but no Christ. There would be positive thinking and inspirational stories, but no Christ. There would be the external trappings of Christianity, but no internal reality of Christ.

The most diabolical ploy of Satan would be for churches to be bulging at their seams, but no proclamation of Christ and Him crucified. With this deadly silence, people would never learn of Christ. Thus, they could never know or follow Him.

What Barnhouse feared has, in large measure, come to pass in our present day. In countless houses of worship across this nation and around the globe, there is much preaching. But the truth is that there is little proclamation of Christ. There is much empty rhetoric, but little reality of the suffering Savior. These churches preach everything except Christ Himself.

Tragically, too many churches and pulpits have everything *except* the main thing.

A CHRISTLESS CHRISTIANITY

Addressing this growing crisis, Michael Horton has written an alarming book, *Christless Christianity*, that drives home this very point. In this stirring work, Horton poignantly notes that churches have become more and more like the world as their pulpits have become increasingly devoid of Christ. Lamentably, the church has been taken captive by the deadening influences of worldly mantras such as crass pragmatism, self-sufficiency, positive thinking, and the like.

An Obsession with Pragmatism

Horton writes, "The church in America today is so obsessed with being practical, relevant, helpful, successful, and even well-liked that it mirrors the world itself. Aside from the packaging, there is nothing that cannot be found in most churches today that could not be satisfied by any number of secular programs and self-help groups."[1] He calls such popular religion Christless Christianity.

Horton further explains, "The focus still seems to be on us and our activity rather than on God and His work in Jesus Christ."[2] Here, Jesus is a coach with a good game plan for our victory rather than a Savior who has already achieved it for us. Salvation is more a matter of having our best life now than being saved from God's judgment by God Himself. Sound familiar?

In short, both Barnhouse and Horton warn of a Christianity without Christ. Barnhouse feared such an alternative gospel was coming. Horton, regrettably, asserts that it is now here.

The Displacement of Christ

In this present hour, preaching that is devoid of the person and work of Christ is all too often commonplace. Such lifeless words are a snare into which many pulpits have fallen, the deadly trap in which the Lord Jesus is minimized, if not altogether absent. Rather than giving Him the central place of preeminence, Jesus is demoted to the periphery. Instead of being in the spotlight, Christ is left standing in the shadows.

In many pulpits, there is compelling communication that captivates the attention of the listener. There is logical thought with a coherent flow. There is a well-structured outline, an attention-grabbing introduction, and excellent exegesis. There are spellbinding illustrations and relevant applications. There are insightful observations and perfect cross-references. There is even a dramatic conclusion.

But if the sermon fails to exalt and elevate Christ, it has missed the mark. Such preaching has everything except the one thing necessary—the person of Jesus Christ, presented by the power of the Spirit. Sure, the name of Christ may be mentioned. But only in a polite manner. Such speech may even be energetic, exciting, and enthusiastic. But if it is devoid of Christ, it is a mere noisy gong and a clanging cymbal. The sad reality is that these barren pulpits are impotent to save and unable to sanctify.

THE REFORMATION OF THE MODERN PULPIT

What must be recovered in our day is the kind of preaching that God blesses. In every pulpit, the Lord Jesus must be presented as more than a mere infallible teacher and a moral example. To be sure, Christ is both. But He is far more. Pulpits must be myopically focused upon declaring the sinless humanity, sovereign deity, and saving purposes of the Lord Jesus Christ. Otherwise, what comes from pulpits is not preaching, but simply tame religious talk.

Proclaiming the Supremacy of Christ

The problem with many sermons today is not in what is said, but in what is *not* said. Many pulpits mention Christ, but only as a mere "life guru" who stands ready to "coach" us in the game of life. Too many preachers represent Christ as the proverbial genie in a bottle who awaits our beckoning call, grants our every whim, and is ready to fix all our temporal problems.

But, to the contrary, preachers must relentlessly magnify the unrivaled lordship of Jesus Christ and the redeeming work He accomplished upon the cross. All pulpits must passionately declare Christ to be the eternal Son of the living

God, the only Savior of sinners. All preaching must boldly announce Him as the reigning Lord of heaven and earth. He must be fearlessly announced as the One before whom every knee will bow and every tongue will confess. All preaching must assert that *this* Jesus is the final Judge of every human life.

To fulfill this sacred duty, every preacher must proclaim the full counsel of God. Every doctrine in Scripture must be delivered. Every truth must be taught. Every sin must be exposed. Every warning must be issued. And every promise must be offered.

If God is to bless our preaching, the supreme majesty of Jesus Christ Himself must be expounded in our sermons. All the lines of our preaching must intersect at this highest pinnacle—Jesus Christ and Him crucified.

Reclaiming the High Ground

Ascending upward from the divine message of Scripture rises the towering edifice of Mount Calvary. Atop this loftiest peak is raised the cross of the Lord Jesus Christ, casting its shadow over the entire Bible. The central theme of the entire Bible is Jesus Christ, the Redeemer of all who call upon Him.

The entire Old Testament announces the coming of Christ to earth in order to redeem and reign. Then the four Gospel accounts detail and describe His first arrival. Next, the book of Acts records the proclamation of His death, resurrection, and exaltation. Moreover, the epistles define who Jesus is and defend what He accomplished in His life and death. Finally, the book of Revelation declares that this One is coming again in grandeur and glory.

Succinctly stated, Jesus Christ crucified is the unifying theme of all of Scripture.

This high ground *must* be claimed in our preaching. Any other footing is a slippery slope that inevitably descends downward into vain rhetoric and mere words. To the contrary, every pulpit must present a towering vision of the unique person and saving work of Jesus Christ. All preaching must point to His sin-bearing, substitutionary death for sinners. All exposition must lift up this Sacrificial Lamb who became a sin-bearing Substitute for all who believe. Every message must exalt this Christ, who was raised from the dead, exalted to the right hand of God the Father, and entrusted with all authority in heaven and earth.

This must be the heartbeat that throbs in every pulpit. This must be the strong pulse that marks every ministry. If preachers are to be known for anything, they must be known for preaching the Lord Jesus Christ and Him crucified.

A Primer on Preaching

For this reason, I am drawn to what the apostle Paul wrote in 1 Corinthians 2:1-9. These insightful verses are a strategic text on the nature of true preaching. In many ways, this passage stands as a definitive passage on biblical preaching. It speaks pointedly to the priority of gospel-centered, grace-filled preaching. This kind of preaching, as described in these verses, desperately needs to be recovered in this day.

Let's look at what Paul said:

> When I came to you, brethren, I did not come with superiority of speech or of wisdom, proclaiming to you the testimony of God. For I determined to know nothing among you except Jesus Christ, and Him crucified. I was with you in weakness and in fear and in much trembling, and my message and my preaching were not in persuasive words of wisdom, but in demonstration of the Spirit and of power, so that your faith would not rest on the wisdom of men, but on the power of God. Yet we do speak wisdom among those who are mature; a wisdom, however, not of this age nor of the rulers of this age, who are passing away; but we speak God's wisdom in a mystery, the hidden wisdom which God predestined before the ages to our glory; the wisdom which none of the rulers of this age has understood; for if they had understood it they would not have crucified the Lord of glory; but just as it is written, "Things which eye has not seen and ear has not heard, and which have not entered the heart of man, all that God has prepared for those who love Him" (1 Corinthians 2:1-9).

A Journey to Corinth

This pivotal passage points back to the time when Paul first came to the city of Corinth, during his second missionary journey. It was in AD 50 that the apostle arrived at this highly cultured city located on the narrow isthmus between the Aegean and Adriatic seas. A wealthy commercial center, Corinth was a prosperous port city that boasted the best of Greek culture. This cosmopolitan metropolis possessed a famous outdoor theater that could accommodate 20,000 people. Here, some of the most renowned ancient Greek actors, dramatists, and orators gathered to perform. The sophisticated Corinthians were accustomed to the most polished communicators in antiquity.

Before coming to Corinth, Paul had preached in other Greek cities, such as Thessalonica, Berea, and Athens. In each of these places, the apostle had been met by emphatic rejections. When Paul finally arrived in Corinth, he was physically and emotionally drained, having suffered numerous doors slammed in his face. The wear and tear on his body had been great, to say nothing of his spirit.

As a result, Paul could have easily been tempted to rethink his approach to ministry. If ever there was a time to change his strategy, this was surely it. Had the apostle been pragmatically driven, he would have concluded that he needed to try something new. Maybe he should mix it up a bit and attempt to be more culturally relevant. Maybe he should adopt the proven methods of the Greek philosophers in order to gain a hearing in Corinth. Maybe he should borrow from their playbook to win over a crowd. Maybe he should use their highly polished style of delivery in order to plant a church there.

If the apostle Paul were to continue his present approach to preaching, how would he even make a dent in the marketplace at Corinth? Should he resort to a different strategy? Should he deemphasize Christ? Should he tone down his message for these sophisticated ears? Should he adopt an alternate approach, something other than preaching, in order to reach this pagan city? Should he try to be suave in his delivery so that he could reach the people's enlightened minds?

How Paul Came

We are not left to wonder. The Bible records Paul's approach to spreading the gospel in Corinth. We read, "He was reasoning in the synagogue every Sabbath and trying to persuade Jews and Greeks. But when Silas and Timothy came down from Macedonia, Paul began devoting himself completely to the word, solemnly testifying to the Jews that Jesus was the Christ" (Acts 18:4-5). Despite the repeated rejections he had suffered earlier, Paul's strategy for reaching Corinth remained unchanged. The apostle maintained the same approach he had used in other cities. He came proclaiming Christ crucified, doing so in the power of the Holy Spirit.

Such Christ-exalting, cross-centered preaching was not without effect. The leader of the synagogue, Crispus, was soundly converted under Paul's ministry (Acts 18:8). Likewise, many other Corinthians came to believe in Jesus.

So powerful was the reception of the gospel there that the apostle stayed 18 months, an unusually long period of time for his fast-paced itinerant schedule. In this pagan city, a beachhead for the truth had now been established. A church had been birthed, as it were, on the doorsteps of hell. Paul's straightforward preaching of the crucified Christ was used mightily by God.

But after Paul's departure from Corinth, these new believers cooled down in their devotion to Christ. Their zeal waned. Though genuinely converted, these disciples reverted back to their desire for more sophisticated styles of public speaking. With this regression came a return to their previous infatuation with worldly wisdom.

In AD 55, Paul wrote 1 Corinthians to confront these people about their spiritual relapse. At the outset of this epistle, he reminded them of the straightforward manner with which he had preached the gospel to them. He stated, "When I came to you, brethren, I did not come with superiority of speech or of wisdom, proclaiming to you the testimony of God" (1 Corinthians 2:1). This is to say, when he was there, Paul had not attempted to match wits with the great Greek debaters. He did not compromise his message in order to accommodate their cultural tastes. Neither did he cater to the conventional wisdom of their Greek minds. He adamantly refused to cater to them in order to win them.

Instead, Paul did not vary the substance of his message one iota. Neither did he adjust the style of his delivery. The apostle came to Corinth as he did every place, preaching the crucified Christ. The entirety of his ministry could be summarized in this succinct statement: "We proclaim Christ, and Him crucified" (see 1 Corinthians 2:2). Bottom line, the sum and substance of his message was the person and work of Jesus Christ.

A TIMELESS MODEL FOR TODAY

Every faithful expositor must follow this same apostolic pattern. No preacher, regardless of where he serves, is free to reinvent preaching. If pulpits are to know divine blessing, those who stand behind them must follow this timeless example in proclaiming Christ and Him crucified. God will honor the one who honors His Word.

No Matter the Audience

Whether one ministers in a large city or in a small town, whether one is trying to reach the cultural elite or the unlettered and unlearned, whether one is involved in student ministry or senior adult ministry, whether one leads a single adult ministry or teaches a young marrieds class, Christ crucified must be the dominant message. With a clarion voice for all to hear, Jesus Christ must be the resounding note in preaching.

This foundational truth of Christ and Him crucified must be emblazoned upon every preacher's soul. This is what

God demands of every man whom He calls to declare His Word. The predominant theme in preaching must be the person and work of Christ.

Let me ask you: Does this Christ-centered message describe your preaching? Are you known for proclaiming Christ and Him crucified? Is your ministry summed up in this one succinct statement: We preach Christ and Him crucified?

The primacy and centrality of Jesus Christ must be true in every pulpit.

A Beeline to the Cross

One great preacher who proclaimed Christ crucified with unequaled success was the nineteenth-century British minister Charles Haddon Spurgeon. This "Prince of Preachers" believed that Christ must be the centerpiece of every sermon. Whatever his passage, Spurgeon announced, "I take my text and make a beeline to the cross."[3] In other words, every time he stepped into the pulpit, he was relentless to set his unwavering focus upon Christ and Him crucified.

A sermon without Christ, Spurgeon insisted, is a graceless sermon. Such a sermon, he maintained, has no good news to declare:

> A sermon without Christ, it is an awful, a horrible thing.
> It is an empty well; it is a cloud without rain; it is a tree
> twice dead, plucked up by the roots. It is an abominable thing to give men stones for bread and scorpions

for eggs, yet they do so who preach not Jesus. A sermon without Christ! As well talk of a loaf of bread without any flour in it. How can it feed the soul? Men die and perish because Christ is not there.[4]

The Preaching God Honors

Simply put, God the Father honors the preaching that honors His Son. If our proclamation departs from this glorious focus, the blessing of God will be far from it. God will abandon the preaching that abandons Christ.

Let us, therefore, commit ourselves to preaching Christ and Him crucified. As we stand in our pulpits, let us never lose sight of the cross. Let us always preach as though we stand under the shadow of Calvary. Christ crucified must remain the chief subject of all we say.

The main thing is to keep the main thing the main thing—and that, quite simply, is preaching Christ.

2
Slick Schtick

The Prohibition of Worldly Preaching

When I came to you, brethren, I did not come with superiority of speech or of wisdom, proclaiming to you the testimony of God (1 Corinthians 2:1).

To an alarming degree, an increasing amount of preaching these days can only be described as "slick schtick." By this I mean that form of communication in which the preacher has little to say, but tragically, says it very well.

This kind of nominal preaching caters to the listener by replacing exposition with entertainment. It substitutes theology with theatrics. It supplants sound doctrine with sound checks. In this sad exchange, the drama of redemption gives way to just plain dramatics. Such negligible preaching has turned many pulpits into a weekend stage for D-List actors who masquerade as preachers.

What passes for preaching in many of today's pulpits is little more than sermonettes for Christianettes. No doubt you know exactly the kind of preaching to which I am referring—20-minute pep talks filled with shallow clichés, self-help snippets, and bumper-sticker slogans.

Worse than their superficial delivery, though, is their shallow doctrine. Such performances are therapeutic, but rarely theological. They are amusing, but not arresting—clever, but not converting. Their anemic message is so empty that in no way do they declare the biblical text listed in the worship program. Soul-starved listeners are left to ask, "Is this all there is?"

Such spiritual junk food, sadly, has become the main entrée for many emaciated congregations. The result is that countless churches are left weak, worldly, and worse, unconverted. When preaching sinks to the low level of being little more than trendy talks about temporal trivialities, the spiritual life of the congregation is in triage. The people stand in desperate need of being rushed to the emergency room and put on life support.

Nothing New in Preaching

Superficial preaching like this is nothing new. This was what the church in Corinth wanted from the apostle Paul. Shaped by the culture of the day, the Corinthians longed for an entertaining orator to fill their pulpit. They demanded smooth-talking actors and communicators who could win them over with their personal panache.

The ancient Roman world was inundated by Greek culture, in which the primary form of entertainment was the commanding delivery of their public speakers. These golden-tongued orators were the celebrities of their day.

They were the icons of the first-century world. Their eloquent speech was regarded to be the crown jewel of the Greek culture. To them belonged the highest pedestals of an adoring populace.

For the citizens in Corinth, public rhetoric was something lofty and noble, something almost godlike. It was a refined form of artistic expression that replaced the savage violence of gladiatorial fights and barbaric sports. The craft of public speaking intentionally sought to secure a specific and desired response from the audience. This was the world in which the Corinthians had been raised. And this was what they insisted upon from the pulpit.

Resisting the Culture

All too often, the same can be said of contemporary preaching. The modern sermon has tragically been described as a mile wide and an inch deep. Others have said today's preacher is a mild-mannered man who urges his mild-mannered listeners to keep being mild-mannered.

The church today would do well to heed Paul's warning to the Christians in Corinth. In this present hour, preachers must resist the temptation to be shaped by the cultural mandates of a godless society. Carnal ears will always want to be charmed and not confronted, captivated and not challenged. Those who stand in pulpits must not cave in to these demands, but maintain the apostolic standard of preaching. This model is permanently etched in stone in the inspired text before us.

Challenges in Corinth

Paul faced many difficulties within Corinth. In one way or another, each was due to this clash with Greek culture. Beneath these issues lay the unmet expectations of the Corinthian congregation. When the apostle first proclaimed the gospel in Corinth, a sizable group responded in faith to Jesus Christ (Acts 18:8-11). But soon after his departure, the attitude that many within the church had toward Paul began to sour. The core problem revolved around both the substance and style of the apostle's preaching.

Clamoring for an Orator

By the elite standards of ancient oratory, Paul was hardly an imposing figure. The Corinthians were accustomed to the *euglottia* from their orators—the beautiful speech. For example, it was said of one such popular speaker, Favorinus, that his eloquence was both *sophos* ("wise") and *potiuos* ("sweet, pleasant"). He reportedly allured his audiences with the intonation and inflection of his voice. He captivated them with the glance of his eyes and the cadence of his speech. It took a highly skilled speaker to impress these enlightened Corinthians.

But Paul fell woefully short of what the Corinthians desired. The apostle lacked the high-octane delivery that fueled a compelling style. He was without the irresistible phrases of typical Greek eloquence. He was deficient in the sophisticated word choices to which they were accustomed.

Paul lacked the proper diction and voice trajectory to move a Greco-Roman crowd to tears or laughter. He seemed wanting in personal charm and magnetic appeal.

Even Paul's physical appearance, they felt, was unimpressive. He was not much to look at. He simply did not measure up to what the Corinthians wanted in a public speaker. In their eyes, this itinerant preacher was out of his league in their worldly wise city.

Savoring the Smooth Talker

What compounded this problem yet further was the fact Paul was followed in pastoral ministry in Corinth by Apollos, "an eloquent man" (Acts 18:24). By all accounts, Apollos was much more polished than Paul in his preaching style. In short order, this speaker had won over the hearts of the Corinthians in a way that Paul had not. Such an infatuation with Apollos only caused further divisions in the church, as many were now saying, "I [am] of Apollos" (1 Corinthians 1:12). Paul knew that if he returned to Corinth, the people would probably be hesitant to commend him to their neighbors and friends.

Because Paul lacked what the Corinthians expected when it came to delivery, they marginalized his doctrine. They could not get past his no-frills, straightforward style of presentation. As a result, they failed to give serious consideration to the substance of his preaching. Consequently, the Corinthians remained carnally minded and spiritually immature. Paul lamented this fact, saying that he could only speak to them as "infants in Christ" (1 Corinthians 3:1-2). That is, he could not give them the meat of the Word, but only the milk.

This led Paul to address their obsession with lofty speech. This worldly fixation was stunting their spiritual growth in grace. They had fallen prey to pursuing style over substance and delivery over doctrine. Thus, their development in true godliness was being severely restricted. A low ceiling was erected over the church in Corinth, hindering the people's maturation upward into Christlikeness.

A Problem That Remains Today

This stiff challenge that Paul faced in Corinth is exactly what many preachers face today. Those who stand in pulpits are being pressured to conform to listeners' entertainment-crazed expectations. They are being tempted to cave in to the desire to be popular in the eyes of the world. They feel the lure to alter their style of presentation and adjust their message in order to find acceptance in the culture around them.

Instead, preachers must remain firmly committed to proclaiming *what* God has said in His Word. Moreover, they must present it *how* the Scripture indicates God's truth is to be presented, regardless of what the culture dictates. While there will be differences in delivery from one preacher to another, there are reasonable limits to which a minister may vary from the acceptable norm outlined in the Word.

Anyone called by God to preach must maintain certain restraints in his delivery so that he does not compromise the message. In short, the medium *does* affect the message.

Martyn Lloyd-Jones, a longtime minister in London, resisted all pressures to adapt his preaching to the whim of the times. In reflecting upon his approach to the pulpit, the Doctor used an analogy drawn from his previous profession as a physician. When challenged to be more compatible with modern thinking, Lloyd-Jones asserted, "I never let the patient write the prescription."[5] By this he meant that he never allowed his listeners to dictate what or how he preached.

How *Not* to Preach

In describing his own preaching, Paul began with a strong negative denial. He emphatically asserted how he did *not* come to Corinth. The apostle said, "I did not come with superiority of speech or of wisdom, proclaiming to you the testimony of God" (1 Corinthians 2:1). These words look back to the time of Paul's earlier visit to Corinth on his second missionary journey. Reflecting on this initial encounter, the apostle adamantly denies having proclaimed a worldly message. Neither did he resort to the inferior methods of a worldly delivery, methods which the Corinthians so relished.

If ever there was a city in which to utilize these two rhetorical devices—"superiority of speech" and "wisdom"—

it was the city of Corinth. These rhetoric-crazed citizens applauded superior oratorical skills. They were mesmerized by the public proclamation of human wisdom. If only Paul had come armed with these two speaking weapons, he could have easily captured the attention of the city. Large crowds would have rushed to hear him. He would have easily played to packed houses.

If Paul had gone door-to-door in Corinth, surveyed the people, and asked them what they desired in a church, they would have enthusiastically responded, "Give us superiority of speech and wisdom, and we will come." They flocked to hear those speakers who employed these popular devices.

But Paul did not resort to such empty tactics. He flatly refused to employ worldly techniques in an attempt to gain an audience. This is *not* the manner in which he presented the gospel to the people in Corinth.

Neither may any preacher today yield to such a compromise. A reliance upon fleshly methods is out of bounds for those whom God commissions. This substandard manner of delivery is unequivocally forbidden to all servants of God. The blessing of heaven will not accompany the preaching that is done in a worldly manner.

Not with Superiority of Speech

When Paul mentioned "superiority of speech," he was referring to worldly techniques in public speech. Specifically, he had in mind those methods gleaned from the

Greek orators of his day. Only 45 miles from Corinth lay the city of Athens—the fountainhead of Greek philosophy and the epicenter of its refined culture. This is where the great philosophers were born and lived. This is where the great orators learned their speaking skills. Because of its close proximity, what was birthed in Athens soon played on Broadway in Corinth.

Lofty Speech Rejected

The precise meaning of "superiority"—as in "superiority of speech"—is "high" speech. It is a metaphorical reference to the speech that communicates with the use of lofty words or high-sounding rhetoric. We might say today that such a speaker used big words or highfalutin language.

Paul resolutely refused to preach in this way. He asserted, "I did not come speaking over your heads. I did not come parading my intellect with highbrow speech." The apostle emphatically stated that he did not rely upon soaring speech or towering rhetoric to wow them. If that was the source of his appeal, he knew that he would surely lose them to the next dazzling speaker to come to town.

When Paul said he came "not with superiority of speech," he meant that he did not communicate like the Greek orators. He did not butter up his listeners or employ calculated techniques to manipulate people. He did not fall back on rhetorical tactics or trained vocal inflections to hypnotize the easily infatuated Corinthians.

Paul did not lean on learned debate strategies or commanding gestures to make his points. Nor did he utilize flowery eloquence or playacting skills learned in Athens. He did not put on a mask of pretense, as though he was onstage, in order to play a character role. He did not present himself to be someone he was not. Simply put, the apostle did not use the art of crafty speech in order to contrive a response.

No Gimmicks Allowed

Adamantly, Paul said, "You know I did not come tickling your ears like other speakers do. I did not try to exploit you." The apostle obviously did not buy into the tired mantra that so many chant today—while the message stays the same, the method is free to change. To the contrary, Paul maintained that not only is the message set by God, but also the parameters of the delivery. Preachers must *not* rely upon human techniques and cleverness.

Sad to say, preaching is too often a parody of the very approach Paul refused to adopt. The gospel message is slickly "packaged" and smoothly "sold" to "the market" in order to "move the product." In this crass perspective, sinners are viewed as "customers" and preaching as an evangelistic "sales tactic." Sermons are crafted as clever "presentations" designed to "close the deal" with "potential buyers." If need be, preachers will use whatever "consumer friendly" approach they believe will "hook" the "seeker." With this man-centered approach to preaching, the soft-sell method in gospel presentation is in vogue.

Those who view their preaching ministry in this way will resort to all kinds of gospel gimmicks in an attempt to grow their churches.

All this is done to make the pulpit trendy and chic in the hopes of gathering a crowd and a following. The church's leadership has clearly placed their confidence in the gabbiness of the messenger rather than the gravity of the message. But is this what the Scripture commands preachers to do? Is this how God commissions His servants to reach the world? The answer is a resounding no.

Such "superiority of speech" is strictly forbidden by God. When the apostle Paul explained his manner of ministry to the Corinthians, he established a timeless pattern for all preachers in every generation: Here is how men are *not* to preach God's Word. We must refuse such forbidden fruit, which is rotten to the core. Simply put, it matters to God how His Word is presented.

Not with Worldly Wisdom

Beyond his delivery, Paul reminded the Corinthians that his coming was "not with wisdom." Here he was referring to the human wisdom of secular worldviews. He said, "I did not come to you with worldly philosophy." In the ancient world, "wisdom" pertained to Greek philosophy. In fact, the Greek term *philosophia* literally means "the love of wisdom." Such carnal insight attempts to construct a world-view that makes sense of life apart from God.

Paul did not try to spice up his message by quoting Greek philosophers like Homer, Plato, Aristotle, and Socrates. He did not draw upon man-centered perspectives on the world. He refused to add one drop of man's polluted thinking to the crystal-clear purity of the gospel.

When Paul said he refused to resort to human wisdom, he meant that he would not appeal to secular ideologies drawn from Greek philosophies. "Superiority of speech" addresses the *style* of his delivery, and "wisdom" its *substance*. The former speaks of the method of communicating, the latter to the content itself. In other words, "wisdom" is *what* one says, "superiority of speech" is *how* one says it. Paul categorically rejected both.

Human Wisdom Refused

When Paul spoke to the Corinthians, he did not offer the world's diagnosis of man's spiritual condition—that he is either well or sick, but certainly not dead. Neither did he offer the world's prescriptions to cure sin-plagued patients. Worldly medicine will not heal the dead; it will only prolong death. If Paul had practiced such medicine, he would have been guilty in the court of heaven of ministerial malpractice.

Admittedly, Greek philosophy asked many of the right questions regarding life: Where did I come from? Who am I? Where am I going? What is life all about? Why am I here?

What is meaning? What is truth? How can I find happiness? How should I live?

Further, philosophy asked the right questions concerning the afterlife: What is death? Where do I go after death? What happens in dying? Will I be with God? Will I find acceptance with Him?

But the Greek philosophers failed to provide the right answers to such life-probing questions. Drawing upon their own limited insight, they gave worldly perspectives, much like many preachers do in this hour.

Paul sharply condemned this corrupt approach in preaching. To the Corinthians the apostle asserted, "I did *not* come to you in such a way. I did *not* give you a worldly diagnosis of your problems." To the contrary, Paul had absolutely nothing to say apart from the Word of God. His lips spoke only what God had entrusted to him. The culture offered him nothing worth proclaiming or believing. Instead, the apostle drew exclusively from divine wisdom in his preaching.

THE WISDOM THAT DIVIDES

Paul was faithful to preach salvation in Christ *alone*. There was no stuttering in his voice. No stammering in his words. Not about this nonnegotiable truth. His message was loud and clear. The sin-bearing death of Christ was the dominant theme in his preaching. The cross was the chief subject of his ministry. The saving work of Christ in His substitutionary death was the central thrust of his doctrine.

To the people in Paul's day, the cross was sheer folly. The message of salvation in Christ alone was considered foolishness by many—even in the church. We can understand such a spiritually blind response from the world. But not from the church! Yet that is what Paul was facing.

To those who truly believe, Paul states that Christ crucified is both the power and wisdom of God. In the previous chapter, he writes, "The word of the cross is foolishness to those who are perishing, but to us who are being saved it is the power of God" (1 Corinthians 1:18). According to this text, the cross is the dividing line of all humanity. The message of Christ crucified separates the human race into two distinct groups. Every person in the world is either perishing or being saved. This great divide created by the cross must be the dominant message of every true preacher.

God's Contempt of Human Wisdom

As Paul unfolded his argument, he announced God's utter disdain of human wisdom. The apostle quoted Isaiah 29:14, in which God Himself is the speaker. He declared, "It is written, 'I will destroy the wisdom of the wise, and the cleverness of the clever I will set aside'" (1 Corinthians 1:19). In no uncertain terms, Paul denounced all human wisdom that seeks to replace or supplement divine revelation. Any such rival wisdom will *not* be tolerated by God.

To be sure, these two schools of wisdom—one of God, the other the world—cannot coexist, but are contrary to one another. God despises the wisdom of this world. He is at complete odds with man's love affair with his own rationale. Here, God vows that He will bring all humanistic thinking to nothingness. He has already judged such wisdom and placed it under His condemnation. The Lord will expose all secular mind-sets for what they are—nothing but damning lies.

In their arrogant insanity, men claim that they are wiser than God by asserting their own thinking and approach to life. And those who listen to them flock to the broken cisterns of their humanistic philosophy in search for the answers to life. But all they discover is empty reservoirs that mock their thirst.

All man-made wisdom is foolish and damning. And God exposes the sheer folly of it. What appears to be foolishness in the cross is, in reality, infinitely wiser than the wisest men in their own thinking. The apparent weakness of Christ crucified is stronger than what the strongest men can offer in their own thinking. By the preaching of the cross, God destroys the wisdom of the wise. By Christ crucified, He sets aside the cleverness of the clever.

God Mocks the Wise

The infinite genius of God in the cross caused Paul to taunt the wise men of this world. The apostle chided them,

"Where is the wise man? Where is the scribe? Where is the debater of this age?" (1 Corinthians 1:20). These rhetorical questions imply answers so obvious that he did not need to answer them. There is not a self-appointed sage in this world who can counter the stunning genius of God in the cross. No one can match wits with the absolute brilliance of God.

All man's ideologies are spiritually bankrupt. They are impoverished in their inability to save. God alone is the Author of saving wisdom. Every preacher must be deeply persuaded of this reality, or he has no right to the pulpit. He must preach God's truth in the gospel, or he is an instrument in the damnation of men's souls.

Without hesitation or timidity, Paul escalated his assault on worldly wisdom. He boldly asserted, "In the wisdom of God the world through its wisdom did not come to know God" (1 Corinthians 1:21). By this, Paul declared that man's wisdom can never lead anyone to God. Human wisdom is a broad path to destruction, never the narrow way to life. Any religion without the exclusivity of the cross leads only to eternal judgment. In their inane foolishness, sinful men are perishing in unbelief.

Paul then acknowledged the two kinds of unbelievers who were refusing the cross in his day. First, the religious Jews wanted a power religion. They longed for a Messiah who was a miracle-working deliverer. They desired a political leader who would break the yoke of Roman oppression. Paul said, "For indeed Jews ask for signs" (1 Corinthians

1:22). Israel looked for one who would restore their nation to its theocratic state. They looked for one who would usher in political stability and independence from Rome. The last thing they wanted was a Savior from sin and judgment.

Further, Paul explained that the Gentiles wanted a brilliant philosophy. He wrote, "Greeks search for wisdom" (1 Corinthians 1:22). That is, the Gentile world was looking for a new worldview. They wanted a new approach to life. They were intrigued with creative ways of looking at the world. They wanted to be intellectually stimulated by a new philosophy.

But they had no interest in a Savior, certainly not one who could save them from divine wrath. Despite their fleshly craving, Paul refused to give them what they wanted. Instead, he remained true to the gospel and preached the cross.

The Empty Deception of Philosophy

Elsewhere, Paul warned believers against adopting any form of human wisdom: "See to it that no one takes you captive through philosophy and empty deception, according to the tradition of men, according to the elementary principles of the world, rather than according to Christ" (Colossians 2:8). Philosophy must be entirely avoided, the apostle admonished, because it ensnares its followers with "empty deception." Humanistic approaches to life may seem profound, but, in reality, they are nothing more than a mere restatement of the elementary principles of the world's empty thinking.

Such self-conceived worldviews, Paul wrote, are "according to the tradition of men." Its secular mind-set is nothing more than man's blind reasoning perpetuated from one generation to the next. It is the same old poison, but with a new label. Of this deception, Solomon wrote, "There is a way which seems right to a man, but its end is the way of death" (Proverbs 14:12). Human philosophy always leads to spiritual death and eternal destruction—no exceptions.

Proclaiming the Testimony of God

Despite the Corinthians' clamoring for wisdom, Paul refused to meet their demands. Instead, the apostle insisted upon proclaiming exclusively the divine revelation in the cross. He remained steadfast and faithful to the eternal message, which he identified as "the testimony of God" (1 Corinthians 2:1). The power, Paul asserted, is in the profound truth of the cross.

Rather than ape their cultural messages, Paul came to Corinth proclaiming the testimony of God. The apostle was concerned for both the *style* ("proclaiming") and the *substance* ("the testimony of God") of what God required in his preaching ministry. "Proclaiming" the message describes the *manner* with which he delivered the truth. Paul came to Corinth and forcefully declared God's message of salvation. In stark contrast to those who offered worldly philosophies, he came proclaiming the unadulterated truth of heaven. In no way did he resort to "superiority of speech."

The gospel is to be declared in all its purity, not diluted with man's wisdom.

Rather than prescribing human opinions, Paul proclaimed "the testimony of God." He declared the unvarnished truth from God Himself. The apostle saw himself as merely a mouthpiece for what God had to say.

WHATEVER HAPPENED TO GOSPEL PREACHING?

As we look around, this seems to be an immensely successful day for gospel preaching. After all, megachurches are thriving far and wide. Some houses of worship boast attendances in excess of 20,000 people per week. One such bulging congregation has even found sanctuary in an NBA arena. Christian conferences are selling out large stadiums for evenings of teaching. Christian television beams broadcasts all around the world by satellite. It would seem that preaching has more clout than ever before.

Not All Is Gold

Yet the church today is not as healthy as she might initially appear. Not all that glitters is gold. Peeling back this thin veneer of evangelical popularity, James Montgomery Boice wrote, "Evangelicalism is seriously off-base today because it has abandoned its evangelical truth-heritage... Instead of trying to do God's work in God's way, it is trying to build a prosperous earthly kingdom with secular tools."[6] Such is the impotence of human wisdom in the modern pulpit.

The Word Did It All

What a contrast this is to what happened during the Reformation, which spread across Europe during the sixteenth century and turned the continent upside down. Kingdoms were tottering. Rome was shaking. The church was awakening. Martin Luther was asked to explain this success. The great Reformer replied with an unwavering confidence in the power of God's Word. He declared, "I simply taught, preached, and wrote God's Word; otherwise I did nothing. And while I slept...the Word so greatly weakened the papacy that no prince or emperor ever inflicted such losses upon it. I did nothing; the Word did everything."[7] This movement, he said, was founded upon the unshakable footing of God's truth.

Nothing has changed in the last 500 years. In this present hour, preachers must still rely exclusively upon the power of God's Word in their ministry. Is this your confidence as you serve the Lord? Are you trusting solely in the testimony of God in your preaching? If so, you stand in good company. You are aligned with the apostle Paul and countless others who shook this world for God.

THE NEED OF THE HOUR

Let me be clear: It matters to God *what* is preached. And it matters to Him *how* it is preached. No man is free to preach whatever and however he so chooses. Every divinely appointed messenger is under a strict mandate to present the truth in a manner that squares with what Paul stated in 1 Corinthians 2:1-9.

The kind of preaching God blesses involves the proclamation of "the testimony of God." There is no place in the pulpit for "superiority of speech." Neither is there any place for man's wisdom. A fleshly message given with a fleshly delivery must, at all costs, be rejected. The gospel must never be trivialized by fleshly proclamations.

Let us not cater to the times in which we live. Rather, let us boldly preach the Word. Let us not rely upon human gimmicks. Instead, let us rest in the saving power of the gospel itself.

3
One Master Theme

The Preeminence of Christ in Preaching

*I determined to know nothing among you except Jesus Christ, and
Him crucified (1 Corinthians 2:2).*

In all preaching, there must be one master theme. From
every pulpit, there must be one dominant note that
resounds. In every message, there must be one central truth
expounded. In one way or another, this underlying truth
must be Christ and Him crucified. The Lord Jesus Christ
alone must have the central place in every sermon.

The essence of Christianity is centered upon the Lord
Jesus Christ. The sum and substance of being a Christian is
trusting Christ with the entirety of one's being. The height
of the Christian life is adoring Christ, the depth of it loving
Him, the breadth of it obeying Him, and the length of it following Him. Everything in the Christian life revolves around
Jesus Christ. Simply put, Christianity *is* Christ.

A SINGULAR FOCUS

The entire Bible is focused on the Lord Jesus Christ,
who came into the world to save sinners. From cover to

cover, all of Scripture speaks with one voice about the primacy of His saving death. This is the strong heartbeat of both the Old and New Testament, pumping divine life into people's souls. To preach the Bible means, chiefly, to preach Christ and Him crucified.

Christ Dominant in Preaching

Because Christ is preeminent throughout Scripture, He must be foremost in biblical preaching. To preach the Bible rightly necessitates proclaiming Christ faithfully. To faithfully proclaim the written Word demands that we preach the living Word. All biblical preaching must declare Christ as its dominant theme. Because the Bible is so Christ-centered, true preaching must likewise be Christ-centered.

With this in mind, Paul explains that the overriding theme of his preaching is Christ and Him crucified. The cross is the sum and substance of the apostle's theology and preaching. Such a Christ-centered focus is the mandate of everyone who steps into a pulpit. In all preaching, Christ *must* be the chief subject.

This is Paul's emphasis in 1 Corinthians 2:1-9. Having already considered verse 1 in the last chapter, let us proceed to verse 2.

THE MESSAGE PAUL DELIVERED

In verse 2, Paul asserted, "I determined to know nothing among you except Jesus Christ, and Him crucified." By this statement, Paul maintained that he was firmly resolved to be Christ-centered in his preaching. He could not be turned aside to a lesser subject. He did not care what his audience desired. Regardless of their whims, Paul gave them Christ.

Paul was not preoccupied with how he was received by the various cities on his missionary journeys. Nor was he concerned about the popular opinions or the perceptions of others. In the face of dissenting voices, the apostle remained unwaveringly determined to preach Christ crucified.

A One-Track Mind

Paul's myopic focus is captured in this one word: "determined" (Greek, *krino*), which means "to judge in a solemn judicial manner." It carries the idea "to render a verdict," or "to pass sentence." In this context, "determined" means that Paul had issued a fixed verdict to pursue this course of action. He was steadfastly resolved and firmly anchored. He had set his mind to preach Christ. From this message he could not be diverted.

When Paul said "except," he meant that he preached nothing *except* Jesus Christ and the centrality of His cross. The essence of his preaching among the Corinthians was Jesus Christ and Him crucified. To be sure, Paul preached "the whole purpose of God" (Acts 20:27), disclosing all the doctrines that God had revealed to him. Yet he said, "I know nothing among you except Jesus Christ, and Him crucified." Every area of divine truth revealed to him was rooted and grounded in the primacy of Christ crucified.

Implied in this statement is that Paul knew nothing of the human wisdom of the Greek philosophers. He did not mimic the worldly mantra of humanistic philosophy. He never proclaimed human psychology or human sociology. Nor did he declare secular humanism or comparative religion. He knew nothing of positive thinking or motivational talks. Paul determined to know nothing except Jesus Christ and Him crucified.

A Singular Focus in Preaching

With fixed determination, Paul came to Corinth with the sole purpose of making known the crucified Son of God, Jesus Christ. He succinctly stated his primary message in the opening chapter of 1 Corinthians when he said, "We preach Christ crucified" (1:23). Unashamedly, he announced that the center of gravity for his preaching is the saving death of Jesus Christ. Though this message is offensive to the unbelieving mind, it is glorious to all who believe. Though it is foolish to the Corinthians, the cross is the power of God unto salvation to all who commit their lives to Christ.

Preaching Christ and Him crucified means proclaiming the person of Christ and the power of His death. Such a declaration magnifies the sufficiency of His vicarious death in saving sinners. No other emphasis in preaching should be allowed to detract from this foremost truth that Jesus accomplished salvation in His sacrifice for sinners. By His atoning death, Jesus has redeemed all who put their trust in Him.

By His vicarious death, Jesus did not merely make salvation hypothetically possible based upon man's response. He *actually* saved a definite number of sinners. True preaching declares the cross as the only way of salvation. Those in bondage to sin have been redeemed by the blood of Christ.

Such preaching constantly unveils the attributes of God in the death of Christ. Such preaching exalts the sovereignty of God in the death of His Son. All preaching must boldly proclaim that holy God is reconciled to sinful men through the blood of the Lamb.

The Dominant Theme

Martin Luther was committed to this kind of straightforward preaching. The focal point of his preaching was the truth that salvation is *solus Christus*—in Christ alone. He maintained, "I preach as though Christ were crucified yesterday, rose from the dead today, and is coming back to earth again tomorrow!"[8] He relentlessly preached Christ in his exposition of Scripture.

Many people commonly associate Luther's preaching with the book of Romans and justification by faith. However, this powerful figure preached only 30 sermons on this epistle. What many people don't know is that this champion of the faith preached more than 1000 sermons on the Synoptic Gospels—sermons which focused directly upon Christ. In addition, he delivered hundreds more from the Gospel of John. The fact is, Luther preached more on

John's Gospel in one year than he did on Romans in the entirety of his ministry.

What could explain such a strong emphasis upon Christ in Luther's preaching?

Luther realized that the four Gospels were an inexhaustible storehouse of truth revealing the Lord and Savior Jesus Christ. He wrote, "We preach always Him, the true God and man who died for our sins, and rose again for our justification. This may seem a limited and monotonous subject, likely to be soon exhausted, but we are never at the end of it."[9] Luther knew that preaching Christ was a limitless subject.

On another occasion, Luther asserted, "The preachers have no other office than to preach the clear Son, Christ. Let them take care that they preach thus, or let them be silent."[10] By this, Luther revealed that he gloried in presenting Christ in His person and work. He had nothing to say apart from Jesus Christ. Any sermon that failed to present Christ failed miserably.

If there is to be a new Reformation in this day, there must be a reformation of the pulpit. Such a restoration will involve restoring Christ to be the chief focus in the pulpit. There must be a decisive return to making Christ the focal point of all preaching.

PREACHING CHRIST CRUCIFIED

For Paul, preaching Christ crucified meant that he must declare the person of Christ as fully God, fully man. At the same time, Paul preached Christ's saving work at the cross. This was the message entrusted to him by God. From it he never deviated to a different message, nor to a contrary emphasis. To this gospel truth he remained true.

The Supreme Person of Christ

In 1 Corinthians 2:2, Paul succinctly stated that he preached "Jesus Christ." Specifically, this proclamation included declaring that Jesus is the eternal Son of the living God, the uncreated Creator who brought into being everything out of nothing. Paul taught that Jesus possesses all the divine attributes that belong exclusively to God. Being fully God, Jesus is coequal and coeternal with God the Father and God the Spirit.

Moreover, the apostle taught that Jesus took upon Himself sinless humanity in His virgin birth. Conceived by the Holy Spirit in Mary, Jesus became the God-man, yet without sin.

Paul preached that Jesus, during His earthly days, lived under the law (Galatians 4:4) and kept it perfectly. He was the perfect model of all righteousness. He was the great prophet promised by Moses (Deuteronomy 18:15), the greatest expositor of the law. In His public ministry, He was demonstrated to be the Son of God by many miracles, signs, and wonders (Acts 2:22).

To be sure, proclaiming the glorious person of Christ was the heart of Paul's preaching.

The Saving Work of Christ

Paul was also faithful to proclaim the saving work of Christ upon the cross. The apostle announced that Jesus made a perfect sacrifice for man's sins as He became a curse for sinners (Galatians 3:13). He taught that the saving death of Christ upon the cross was sufficient for all who will call upon His name.

The eternal benefits of the death of Jesus are "wisdom from God, and righteousness and sanctification, and redemption" (1 Corinthians 1:30). This is to say, the wisdom of the cross declares that Christ provided perfect righteousness, cleansing sanctification, and redemption from bondage to sin and Satan. As a steward of God, Paul was under divine mandate to preach these truths with unwavering devotion. He was to resist any distraction that would pull him in another direction. He was to never deviate from the cross.

Is Jesus Christ the dominant theme in your preaching? In the pulpit, do you magnify His sovereign lordship and saving work? In your ministry, do you continually point your listeners to Him? Do you call people to commit their lives to Him?

A FAITHFUL MESSENGER

As a preacher, Paul was a divinely appointed herald of Christ crucified. Being a herald is entirely different than being an orator. A herald is judged solely on the basis of faithfully delivering the message exactly as it has been entrusted to him. He is not responsible for the response of the listener. Rather, his job is to faithfully dispatch his message.

While an orator is measured by the response he is able to elicit from his listeners, this is not the case with a herald. An orator is results-driven, whereas a herald is message-driven.

A Spokesman for His Master

As defined by Gustav Friedrich in the *Theological Dictionary of the New Testament*, a herald (Greek, *keryx*) is one who is faithful to deliver his message exactly as it is given to him. Friedrich writes:

> The essential point about the report which they give is that it does not originate with them. Behind it stands a higher power. The herald does not express his own views. He is the spokesman for his master…Heralds adopt the mind of those who commission them, and act with the plenipotentiary authority of their masters…In the main, the herald simply gives short messages, puts questions, and brings answers…He is bound by the precise instructions of the one who commissions him.[11]

In carrying out his mission, the reliable herald must never become sidetracked. He is to simply announce his message, and then return to his dispatching sovereign for further orders. Concerning the role of a herald, Friedrich explains:

The good herald does not become involved in lengthy negotiations, but returns at once when he has delivered his message…[I]n general, he is simply an executive instrument. Being only the mouth of his master, he must not falsify the message entrusted to him by additions of his own. He must deliver it exactly as given to him…[H]e must keep strictly to the words and orders of his master.[12]

This is precisely how Paul saw himself. He was a herald who must strictly adhere to the message given to him. God had commissioned him with the message of Christ crucified. This truth he must proclaim. Despite the expectations of the Corinthians, Paul understood that he must not reshape the message in order to make it more appealing in the hopes of winning over his audience. For the apostle, the gospel message was permanently etched in stone.

Paul knew he could not alter his message or manipulate his listeners to achieve some desirable effect. He was to deliver what had been given to him, and leave the results to his Master.

Leaving the Results with God

Upon delivering his message, a herald will encounter a variety of responses from his audience. But these are not to be his concern. Despite whatever acceptance the herald might personally desire from his listeners, he must not allow the desired result to affect his delivery.

It's important to recognize that ultimately, an audience's response to a message reflects their attitude toward the *sender* of the message, not the messenger himself. Under no circumstances can a herald alter his message in order to gain a better response. Neither can he negotiate the message in order to make it more palatable.

The implications of this are that a herald cannot be success-driven. Instead, he is to be obedience-driven. He is an enlisted man under orders from his sovereign. His task is narrowly restricted to announcing the content of his message and declaring the response necessary from his listeners. Instead of presenting a litany of persuasive arguments, he is to declare the message given to him, and report back to the one who commissioned him.

With that in mind, Paul found it necessary to correct the Corinthians' flawed view of a preacher. If he did not rectify this misperception, their Christian lives would remain carnal and immature. Further, their church would be stagnated.

As a herald, Paul knew that he must deliver the message God gave to him and leave the results with the Lord. It did not matter if Paul was misunderstood by some, or scorned by others. He had to accept this role and carry out his sacred duty. It was not the Corinthians to whom he had to answer. Rather, he had to give an account to God Himself.

This is the strict accountability that every preacher has to God. Every herald who steps into a pulpit is directly responsible to the One who commissioned him to the task. If you please God, it does not matter whom you displease. And if you displease Him, it does not matter whom you please.

The Division of the Cross

In 1 Corinthians 1:18, Paul said, "The word of the cross is foolishness to those who are perishing, but to us who are being saved it is the power of God." By this, Paul meant that the cross divides all humanity into only two groups. To the unbeliever, the cross is foolishness. But to the believer, it is the power of God. The cross separates the people of the world into those two categories.

Foolishness to the World

Paul said that the gospel is "foolishness" to the unsaved. This is a word (Greek, *moros*) from which we derive the English word *moron*. It refers to one without the intellectual ability to process information and draw right conclusions. Paul asserts that, to the unconverted mind, the truth regarding a crucified Savior is moronic, irrational, and illogical. The proclamation of the death of Christ is thought to be idiotic and unintelligent, even insane madness.

Regarding this foolishness, Paul wrote, "A natural man does not accept the things of the Spirit of God, for they are foolishness to him; and he cannot understand them, because they are spiritually appraised" (1 Corinthians 2:14). This is to say, the preaching of the cross remains unintelligent to the natural man, who has experienced only a natural birth, not a spiritual one.

The preaching of the cross is always foolishness to the unsaved world. Yet many contemporary preachers do not want their message to be nonsense to the unconverted. Longing to be accepted, they turn to "superiority of speech" in order to gain popularity. They adopt the world's wisdom to gather an audience. Tragically, they cannot accept that the cross is sheer foolishness to the world.

By contrast, "To us who are being saved it [the cross] is the power of God" (1 Corinthians 1:18). Those whose eyes have been opened by grace see the cross in an entirely different way. No longer in darkness, they view the cross for what it is—the means of salvation from divine wrath.

A Stumbling Block to Jews

Paul said, "We preach Christ crucified, to Jews a stumbling block" (1 Corinthians 1:23). The religious Jews of Jesus' day wanted a powerful deliverer who would free them from the oppression of the foreign nations. They longed for one who would rescue them from the tyranny of the Roman Empire. They had no interest in a crucified Messiah.

To the Jew, the message of a murdered Messiah was the ultimate scandal. In Roman times, crucifixion was a punishment reserved for the worst criminals. So dreaded was death by crucifixion that no Roman citizen could be nailed to a cross. Such a horrific death was reserved for the notorious enemies of the Empire—terrorists, murderers, and anarchists.

When the Jews were told that their long-awaited Messiah had been put to death on a cross, this was a stumbling block to them—literally, a scandal. It was a scorned message of defeat, not victory, that caused them to fall further into unbelief.

Yet Paul did not alter his message from the cross. Israel's rejection of Christ did not cause him to adopt a different approach in preaching. Though Christ and Him crucified was a stumbling block to the Jews, Paul nevertheless preached it faithfully, even forcibly.

There is no gospel preaching apart from preaching Christ crucified. The proclamation of the cross will always be a stumbling block to those who are religious but lost. To them, the cross is foolishness.

SERMONS FULL OF CHRIST

The inauguration service of the Metropolitan Tabernacle in London in 1861 was a great moment in church history. On this monumental occasion, Charles Haddon Spurgeon, only 26 years old, ascended the pulpit to preach his first sermon in that structure. Spurgeon spoke on what was the grandest theme of his entire preaching ministry—Jesus Christ.

The Chief Subject of Ministry

As Spurgeon announced his text, he proclaimed, "Daily in the temple, and in every house, they ceased not to teach and preach Jesus Christ" (Acts 5:42 KJV). By this, Spurgeon declared what he believed must be the central focus of his ministry in this newly constructed house of worship. Christ must always be the heart of any declaration. No matter what his text, Spurgeon was relentlessly riveted upon Jesus Christ.

In this inaugural sermon, Spurgeon declared words that should ring true in the heart of every preacher. He asserted:

> I would propose that the subject of the ministry of this house, as long as this platform shall stand, and as long as this house shall be frequented by worshippers, shall be the person of Jesus Christ...if I am asked to say what is my creed, I think I must reply—"It is Jesus Christ"... the body of divinity to which I would pin and bind myself for ever, God helping me, is...Christ Jesus, who is the sum and substance of the gospel; who is in Himself all theology, the incarnation of every precious truth, the all-glorious personal embodiment of the way, the truth, and the life.[13]

By this statement, Spurgeon maintained that all true preaching must have, as its central thrust, the person and work of the Lord Jesus Christ. On another occasion Spurgeon stated, "This is the sum; my brethren, preach CHRIST, always and evermore. He is the whole gospel. His person, offices, and work must be our one great all-comprehending theme."[14] For the preacher, Christ is *everything*.

Preaching the Greatness of Christ

This Christ-centered focus is the standard to which every preacher must adhere, in every generation, in every place. Christ should be magnified in every sermon. We should thrill in the privilege of extolling His name.

Great preachers *always* preach a great Christ. Wherever they may be weak, they must always succeed in proclaiming the matchless greatness of the Lord Jesus. Regardless of the culture in which they serve or the expectations of their listeners, faithful preachers are committed to upholding the unrivaled supremacy of Jesus Christ in His saving death.

In this present hour, may preaching be firmly rooted in Christ and Him crucified. May preachers declare the incomparable person and finished work of the Lord Jesus. May pulpits be singularly marked as always magnifying the glories of His sovereign majesty.

4

Strength in Weakness

The Power of the Spirit in Preaching

*I was with you in weakness and in fear and in much trembling,
and my message and my preaching were not in persuasive words of
wisdom, but in demonstration of the Spirit and of power, so that
your faith would not rest on the wisdom of men, but on the power
of God (1 Corinthians 2:3-5).*

The kind of preaching God blesses is inherently paradoxical.
This is to say, biblical exposition demonstrates a seemingly
apparent contradiction. In the one who preaches, there are
two polar opposites—strength and weakness. This perceived
antinomy is found in this: God's strength is made perfect in
man's weakness. The kind of preaching that heaven blesses
involves a frail messenger being filled by divine might.
It is the preacher who recognizes his own weakness who
relies upon God's grace. It is this messenger who is divinely
empowered to declare His Word.

This is always the divine plan. God delights in using a
fragile messenger to declare His "foolish" message. The one
who humbles himself before God will be exalted to deliver
the good news of Jesus Christ. The one who empties himself will be filled by the Spirit. The one who lowers himself

before God will be lifted up by Him. In his own frailty, the weak preacher is made strong.

DESCENDING INTO GREATNESS

Regarding such weakness, the story is told of a young seminary graduate who eagerly set out to preach his first sermon in his new pastorate. After several years of intense theological study, he was ready to unleash his vast learning upon this unsuspecting congregation. As he entered the pulpit, he did so with an amazing amount of self-assurance. Standing before the people, his chest was pushed forward, his head erect, his countenance glowing.

But as this young theologian delivered his maiden sermon, he unexpectedly began to falter. His tongue became thick. He stumbled over his words. He lost his place in his notes. His concentration was broken. His delivery waned. By all accounts, the sermon was a complete failure.

Immediately after this excruciating experience was over, this devastated young pastor slithered down from the pulpit. His head was low, his shoulders slouched over, his knees weak. Never had he been so humbled by such pride-crushing embarrassment.

As he exited the sanctuary, an older deacon approached him and, putting his arm around him, said, "Pastor, if you had gone up into the pulpit the way you came down, you would have come down the way you went up."

A God-dependence in the Pulpit

Whenever any preacher enters the pulpit relying upon his own strength, he is certain to falter and fail. Concerning man's inability, Jesus said, "Apart from Me you can do nothing" (John 15:5). The preacher is no exception. When he trusts in himself, he will accomplish nothing of eternal significance.

The one who ministers with self-reliance will certainly be ineffective. In a discussion on spiritual leadership, Peter said, "God is opposed to the proud, but gives grace to the humble" (1 Peter 5:5). The preacher who acts self-sufficient will surely be humbled by God. One way or another, he will be humbled. He will either choose to be humble, or he will be humbled. When it comes to the pulpit, there must be a complete dependence upon God to work through the messenger and the message.

When clothed with humility, the preacher is endued with power from on high. Despite any personal weaknesses he might have, the Spirit will enable him to stand strong in proclaiming the Scripture.

This is the humility with which any minister needs to approach the pulpit. Those who recognize their weaknesses are made strong. Those who recognize their inadequacies are made adequate. Those who realize their helplessness receive divine help. This is the sovereign design and infinite genius of God. Finite men must preach in the power that only an infinite God can provide. This is the paradox of preaching.

A Weak Preacher in Corinth

It was in such humility that Paul came to the city of Corinth. The apostle felt the heavy weight of responsibility that came with his God-assigned mission. Far from being self-sufficient, he entered this imposing city with much fear and trembling. Feeling his accountability to God, Paul recognized the enormity of the task and was shaken to the very core of his being.

In the midst of this personal weakness, Paul confided that divine power was given to him. The weaker he was, the stronger he became. The emptier he was, the more he was filled with might. Though Paul appeared in Corinth with much weakness, he preached "in demonstration of the Spirit and of power" (1 Corinthians 2:4).

This paradox must be experienced in every preacher. No man is too weak for God to use, only too strong. The more one recognizes his own weakness, the more he will rely upon God for strength. By His sovereign design, God chooses to use weak vessels whom He makes strong.

Have you come to realize this? Do you recognize your own weakness in preaching Christ? Have you come to see your personal inadequacy in ministry? Are you so filled with such deep concern for the advance of the gospel that you are overcome with much fear and trembling? Hopefully so.

God empowers those who completely rely upon Him. Only those who feel their weakness look to Him for strength. As you step into the pulpit, may you recognize your inadequacies and trust in His all-sufficient grace.

In Much Human Weakness

To be sure, Paul felt his own lack of strength. The apostle reminded the people that when he came to Corinth preaching the gospel, "I was with you in weakness and in fear and in much trembling" (1 Corinthians 2:3). By this, Paul acknowledged that he stood in stark contrast to the Greek orators of his day. He was the polar opposite of these highly-skilled communicators. These silver-tongued speakers certainly did not stand before their audience in a weakened state. These renowned rhetoricians did not exhibit any human frailty or lack self-confidence. Instead, they mesmerized their listeners with their suave style of speech.

Physically Frail, Emotionally Weak

But Paul assumed an entirely different posture. The apostle confessed that he stood before the Corinthians "in weakness and in fear and in much trembling" (1 Corinthians 2:3). The message appeared to be weak to them, and so did the messenger. Paul felt an acute sense of inadequacy when he preached the gospel in this pagan city. Fully aware of Corinth's moral degeneracy, Paul realized the enormity of the challenge before him. He was, no doubt, overwhelmed.

How could the gospel penetrate this secular stronghold? Would Paul adopt the style of his Greek counterparts? To the contrary, the apostle came with no showbiz glitz. No gospel gimmicks. No manipulative methods. He came with the opposite—weakness, fear, and trembling.

By the time Paul entered Corinth, he was reeling under the pressures that he had faced elsewhere. He had been severely beaten and imprisoned in Philippi (Acts 16:19-40), run out of town in Thessalonica (Acts 17:5-10) and Berea (Acts 17:13-14), and scoffed at and ridiculed in Athens (Acts 17:32-33). In short, he was physically weak and emotionally spent.

But no preacher is any stronger than when he is weak. Only then does he trust in the power of the Spirit. In this debilitating state of weakness, Paul would be supernaturally empowered and energized by the Holy Spirit. The apostle would later confess, "I will rather boast about my weaknesses, so that the power of Christ may dwell in me. Therefore I am well content with weaknesses, with insults, with distresses, with persecutions, with difficulties, for Christ's sake; for when I am weak, then I am strong" (2 Corinthians 12:9-10). Here is strength in weakness.

Fear God, Not Man

When Paul said he came "in fear and in much trembling," he did not mean that he was fearful of public speaking. Neither was he implying that he was scared to die, nor that he was fearful of being considered intellectually inferior to the Greek orators. The apostle was not apprehensive about personal rejection.

Rather, Paul's lowly demeanor was the result of the seriousness of his mission. He was humbled by the magnitude of the task ahead of him. Reaching this large city with the gospel weighed heavily upon him. He understood that the souls of men were literally hanging in the balance. This reality sobered him as he preached to perishing individuals in desperate need of salvation.

Anticipating that Final Day

This was the same soul-arresting fear that Paul felt as he preached in Corinth. The apostle understood that there was coming a day when he would give an account to God for his ministry. Scripture gives this warning for every minister: "Let not many of you become teachers, my brethren, knowing that as such we will incur a stricter judgment" (James 3:1). This underscores the seriousness of the preacher's accountability before God.

In 1 Corinthians, Paul cautions:

> Each man's work will become evident; for the day will show it because it is to be revealed with fire, and the fire itself will test the quality of each man's work. If any man's work which he has built on it remains, he will receive a reward. If any man's work is burned up, he will suffer loss; but he himself will be saved, yet so as through fire (3:13-15).

Like a purging fire, God's final judgment will test the quality of each man's ministry and message. With the knowledge of this future final exam before him, Paul faithfully preached.

In 2 Corinthians, Paul reinforces this truth: "We must all appear before the judgment seat of Christ, so that each one may be recompensed for his deeds in the body, according to what he has done, whether good or bad" (5:10). The reality of a future final evaluation kept Paul in much fear and trembling. This sober realization kept a healthy fear of God within his soul.

At a recent pastors' conference, it was shared with me that a man was approached by another pastor who conveyed he had found the success of spiritual leadership. "It really comes down to *swagger*," this pastor said. "When you walk into a room, you have to have a swagger about you."

By this standard, the apostle Paul was an abysmal failure. When he came to Corinth, there was no swagger to his entrance—only shaking. The apostle did not strut before the Corinthians; rather, he came with a holy trepidation.

Such a fear of God is sorely lacking in pulpits today.

Not with Manipulative Speech

Paul then advanced his argument yet further. He explained, "My message and my preaching were not in persuasive words" (1 Corinthians 2:4). By this, the apostle clarified what the content of his doctrine ("my message") and the manner of delivery ("my preaching") were *not*. This twofold nature of preaching refers to both its substance and style. By this strong negative denial, Paul was reminding the Corinthians that he did *not* come to them as did the

Greek orators. That is to say, he did not come with a worldly message, nor in a fleshly manner.

Paul's preaching in Corinth did not generate applause. His sermons were not filled with clever banter and hot-button words designed to captivate his audience. He did not butter up his listeners with false flattery, nor did he tickle their ears to win them to himself. He did not pander to them, nor did he appeal to their flesh. There were no calculated theatrics, no crafty techniques. Paul did not appeal to emotionalism or crude humor. This was *not* how Paul came to Corinth.

The question then begs to be asked: *How* did Paul come? The answer is found in the second half of verse 4.

In Demonstration of Power

Unlike the Greek orators, the apostle's preaching was "in demonstration of the Spirit and of power" (1 Corinthians 2:4). In other words, Paul came to the city of Corinth with an utter reliance upon God. In his personal weakness, the power of God was operating mightily. In his desperation, he was supernaturally energized by the Holy Spirit to preach Jesus Christ and Him crucified.

Evidence of the Spirit's Power

Paul's proclamation of the cross was "in demonstration of the Spirit." This word "demonstration" communicates the idea of presenting irrefutable evidence in a court of law.

It was a technical term, used in rhetoric, for proof given in a compelling speech. But the convincing proof that Paul's preaching displayed was not what the Corinthians wanted. They wanted a show of oratorical skills. Instead, Paul offered a demonstration of the Spirit's power.

What is the precise nature of this "demonstration" of the Spirit's power? Some argue that it refers to signs and miracles performed under Paul's preaching. But this cannot be the intended meaning. Paul had earlier argued *against* the Jews' requests for signs (1 Corinthians 1:22). It would be incongruent for Paul to appeal to what he had just rebuked. Paul's listeners desired an external demonstration of power. But Paul preached with a display of the true power of God— the power of the gospel in Christ crucified.

Indeed, this "demonstration" was seen in the Corinthians' own lives. This power was evidenced in their conversions to Christ. Their being convicted of sin and turning to Christ crucified was undeniable proof of the power of God in Paul's preaching. They could clearly behold the irresistable force of the Spirit in Paul's ministry and message. They simply needed to look at their own lives; the evidence of the Spirit's power was evident *in* themselves.

The Promise of Power

This spiritual power had been promised by Jesus Christ. In the Great Commission, the Lord said, "I am sending forth the promise of My Father upon you; but you are to stay in the city until you are clothed with power from on high" (Luke 24:49). This very same power was with Paul, enabling him to preach the gospel with life-changing effect.

Jesus further stated, "You will receive power when the Holy Spirit has come upon you; and you shall be My witnesses" (Acts 1:8). By this divine power, the apostle was strengthened to give convincing testimony of Christ's substitutionary death.

This sovereign might is what Paul had experienced earlier when he preached in Thessalonica. The apostle asserted, "Our gospel did not come to you in word only, but also in power and in the Holy Spirit and with full conviction" (1 Thessalonians 1:5). That is to say, his preaching was accompanied by a deep power within him—the soul-riveting, inner certainty of the truth in his own mind and heart. Specifically, the Spirit brought him greater assurance of the people's need for Christ and an overwhelming confidence in His power to save them.

Paul asserted this very same power in preaching when he wrote to the church in Colossae: "We proclaim Him, admonishing every man and teaching every man with all wisdom, so that we may present every man complete in Christ. For this purpose also I labor, striving according to His power, which mightily works within me" (Colossians 1:28-29). As Paul proclaimed Christ, the Spirit mightily empowered him.

Martyn Lloyd-Jones noted the absolute necessity of the power of the Spirit in preaching. He explained, "If there is no power it is not preaching. True preaching, after all, is God acting. It is not just a man uttering words; it is God using him. He is being used of God. He is under the influence of the Holy Spirit."[15] Put simply, all true preaching is energized by the power of the Spirit.

As the preacher experiences this power, Lloyd-Jones maintained, "it is God giving power, and enabling, through the Spirit, to the preaching in order that he may do this work in a manner that lifts it up beyond the efforts and endeavors of man to a position in which the preacher is being used by the Spirit and becomes the channel through whom the Spirit works."[16] In other words, authentic preaching involves God working in His messengers, granting true power in the proclamation.

Concerning this divine power, Lloyd-Jones said that the Spirit "gives clarity of thought, clarity of speech, ease of utterance, a great sense of authority and confidence as you are preaching, an awareness of a power not your own, thrilling through the whole of your being and an indescribable sense of joy. You are a man 'possessed,' you are taken hold of, and taken up."[17] Spirit-dominated preaching is a powerful experience.

Moreover, Lloyd-Jones stated, "You have a feeling that you are not actually doing the preaching, you are looking on. You are looking on at yourself in amazement as this is happening. It is not your effort; you are just the instrument, the channel, the vehicle, and the Spirit is using you, and you are looking on in great enjoyment and astonishment."[18]

Passion in the Pulpit

Another manifestation of this power in preaching is a God-given passion for the truth. In Paul's "proclaiming" (1 Corinthians 2:1), there was a divinely-given fervor within him as he preached. When he was filled by the Spirit, he proclaimed the message with deep passion. He felt the truth of his message deep within him. With a fire in his bones, divine energy pulsed through his heart as he preached.

Where there is no passion, there is no *real* preaching. Spurgeon quipped that some ministers "would make good martyrs—that is, they are in need of catching fire." Of one preacher, he said sarcastically, "There was no doubt of his burning well, he was dry."[19] The tragedy is that many pastors are not excited when they proclaim the Word. Where there is a lack of zeal in preaching, it is because there is an absence of power.

John Murray, who taught at Westminster Seminary, emphatically asserted, "Preaching without passion is not preaching at all."[20] In other words, whenever the Holy Spirit is empowering the preacher, there is a God-given zeal in his heart that governs his delivery." To be sure, the Spirit never makes God's messengers dull and dry.

Regarding such inner fire, R.C. Sproul states, "Dispassionate preaching is a lie."[21] This is to say, bland speech from a pulpit is a contradiction in terms. Whatever it is, it is definitely not preaching.

Sproul argues that where there is no passion for the truth, there is no real preaching—only bland rhetoric. But where the Spirit of God is working in power in the preacher, true preaching will result.

Such passion in preaching is desperately needed today. Before there can be a fire in the pew, there must first be a fire in the pulpit.

Power That Gives Urgency

This inherent power in preaching also increases a minister's sense of urgency. When the Spirit emboldens him, there is no casual delivery in the pulpit. The Spirit-filled preacher is not indifferent toward the truth. He does not possess a blasé attitude. Nor is there a cold aloofness within him.

Instead, the Spirit generates an overwhelming passion to reach people with the gospel. The Spirit causes the preacher to burn with intensity as he proclaims Christ.

Noted Puritan Richard Baxter wrote a well-known book titled *The Reformed Pastor*. In this work, Baxter called for a reformed ministry that conforms with Scripture. Biblical preaching, he contended, must come with a sense of explosive urgency. Baxter wrote:

> What! Speak coldly for God, and for men's salvation? Can we believe that our people must be converted or condemned, and yet speak in a drowsy tone? In the name of God, brethren, labour to awaken your own hearts, before you go to the pulpit, that you may be fit to awaken the hearts of sinners. Remember they must be awakened or damned, and that a sleepy preacher will

hardly awaken drowsy sinners. Though you give the holy things of God the highest praises in words, yet, if you do it coldly, you will seem by your manner to unsay what you said in the matter."[22]

Baxter then delivered the knockout punch when he said that, in preaching, "it is a kind of contempt of great things, especially of so great things, to speak of them without affection and fervency."[23] In other words, preaching that lacks urgency lacks the Spirit's power. It is not real preaching.

Whenever the Spirit is at work in the preacher, there is a fervency for Christ and an urgency that the listeners must follow Him. In Spirit-energized preaching, there rages an inner fire in the preacher.

Relying upon the Spirit

Why does God choose to work through the weakness of finite messengers? Paul said, "so that your faith would not rest on the wisdom of men, but on the power of God" (1 Corinthians 2:5). He preached in the Spirit's power so that the Corinthians would trust in God and not in him. He preached in the Spirit's power for the sake of the Corinthians. Rather than persuade them through his cleverness, Paul wanted them to respond to the truth clearly presented.

If Paul had relied upon superiority of speech and worldly wisdom, his listeners, in reality, would have placed their faith in him. The result of personality driven preaching would be false converts who had placed their trust in a man. Such preaching would have produced spurious disciples who professed Christ but did not know Him.

On the other hand, proclaiming Christ in the power of the Spirit brings about an entirely different result. Where the cross is proclaimed, the faith of men rests exclusively in "the power of God." This is the power of the Spirit in preaching. Only then will listeners believe in the Lord Jesus.

If any ministry endeavor is to succeed, the Lord says it must be "not by might nor by power, but by My Spirit" (Zechariah 4:6). If souls are to be saved, the preacher's ability is insufficient. Only the active power of the Holy Spirit can enable the proclamation of the gospel to have converting power.

A dependence upon the Spirit is an absolute necessity for every pastor. It is in his dire weakness that the Spirit makes him strong. In the pulpit, he must prostrate himself before Almighty God in order that He might raise him up. As he dies to self, the Spirit grants power. This is the paradox of preaching.

The Monopoly of the Spirit

In the nineteenth century, a group of pastors were organizing a citywide evangelistic campaign. As they discussed who they should invite to preach, the name of the noted evangelist D.L. Moody was brought up. Reluctant to have

Moody preach, one minister protested, "Why Moody? Does he have a monopoly on the Holy Spirit?"

The question was then followed by a long silence. Finally, another pastor spoke up, saying, "Moody, Moody, Moody...does Moody have a monopoly on the Holy Spirit?" One of the others answered, "No, but it seems that the Holy Spirit has a monopoly on Moody."[24]

No greater point could be made for any preacher.

God works through His servants in whom His Spirit is mightily empowering. Regardless of a preacher's résumé or ministerial credentials, the Holy Spirit is the One who, ultimately, makes the difference in any preacher's ministry.

When it comes to your preaching, does the Holy Spirit have a monopoly on *you*?

Do you know what it is to preach in demonstration of the power of the Spirit? Do you know what it is to be in much trembling and weakness and fear? Do you know what it is to call out to God, pleading for His Spirit to accompany you into the pulpit? Have you witnessed the fullness of His power in your mind, heart, and disposition as you minister the Word?

As you preach the gospel, you must be empowered by the Spirit of God. Your life must be dominated by divine strength from on high. You must be one who knows what it is to preach in the power of the Holy Spirit. Only then will you know what it is to *really* preach.

5

A Sovereign Wisdom

The Predestination of the Father in Preaching

Yet we do speak wisdom among those who are mature; a wisdom, however, not of this age nor of the rulers of this age, who are passing away; but we speak God's wisdom in a mystery, the hidden wisdom which God predestined before the ages to our glory; the wisdom which none of the rulers of this age has understood; for if they had understood it they would not have crucified the Lord of glory; but just as it is written, "Things which eye has not seen and ear has not heard, and which have not entered the heart of man, all that God has prepared for those who love Him"
(1 Corinthians 2:6-9).

There is a foundational truth in preaching that must undergird every message—namely, that God is sovereign over all things. With all Spirit-empowered exposition, God must be proclaimed as the Supreme Ruler over all the affairs of human history. He must be declared as presiding over all events and circumstances in this world. Further, Scripture proclaims that God directs every human life, determining every eternal destiny. Consequently, God's sovereignty must be a dominant note in preaching that handles the Scriptures faithfully.

Nowhere is this kind of preaching more essential than in matters pertaining to salvation. Before man ever fell into sin, God had already foreordained the way by which He would restore their broken relationship. Before sin corrupted the entire human race, God had already predestined the plan of salvation. Before the world became polluted by man's depravity, He had already predetermined the redemption by which He would restore ruined sinners to Himself. More importantly, God even chose His elect upon whom He would freely bestow His unmerited grace.

By sovereign grace, God is the Initiator, never the responder. God is the Seeker, never the one who is sought. God is the Savior, man is the one rescued. God is the Provider, man is the debtor. God is the subject and active verb, man is the object who is acted upon.

From start to finish, every aspect of man's salvation is divinely designed and determined by this foreordination; all glory goes to God alone. This is true wisdom—that God is entirely sovereign in salvation. He is Lord over every detail of every circumstance that brings about this divinely provided salvation.

ALL GLORY TO GOD

Years ago, noted Bible expositor Dr. Harry Ironside told of a man who was giving his testimony before a group, explaining how it was he had come to faith in Christ. This man gave witness of how God had sought him while he was living in sin. He told of how God had loved him while he was still an enemy of the cross. He explained how God had called him out of spiritual darkness to escape divine wrath.

God had delivered him from a life of wretched debauchery. Grace had freely and fully cleansed him from sin's defilements. This testimony was exceptionally powerful because it gave all glory to God.

After the meeting, one listener took the man aside and said, "I appreciate all that you had to say about what God did for you, but you failed to mention anything about your part. After all, salvation is really part us and part God. You should have mentioned something about what you did."

"You are right," the newly converted man replied, "I should have mentioned my side. My part was running away from God as fast as I could, and His part was running after me until He found me."

God, the Seeker of Souls

Ironside's story illustrates the point that long before man fell into sin, God had already predestined His pursuit of individual sinners. Before the foundation of the world, God designed His plan of salvation by which He would rescue His elect. Before time began, He chose His Son to come into this world in order to save these elect who are unable to save themselves. And pulpits everywhere must be faithful in declaring this bedrock truth.

Yet man, left to his own thinking, is constantly seeking to take credit—at least, in part—for that which God alone has accomplished in salvation. Man flatters himself in perceiving that by his own initiative and choice, he chooses to seek after God. He vainly imagines that his pursuit of salvation is other than God first seeking him. But, in truth, it is God alone who seeks and saves.

Divine Sovereignty in Salvation

The kind of preaching God blesses is that which proclaims the sovereignty of God in salvation. Some preachers naively present the notion that man controls his own life and determines his own destiny. Others surmise that Satan and demons are ruling this world. But such preaching turns theology upside down on its head and robs God of His glory.

This kind of man-centered proclamation obscures the fact that God alone reigns in grace. As Scripture says, "For from Him and through Him and to Him are all things. To Him be the glory forever. Amen" (Romans 11:36). By these three prepositions, "from," "through," and "to," "all things" includes every aspect of salvation. God is the Source, the Means, and the Goal of all things. This being so, every pulpit must declare this God-centered reality.

The gospel narrative of sovereign grace is not a recent solution to the problem of sin. The death of Christ was not a divine afterthought. Calvary was not a knee-jerk reaction to fix an unforeseen dilemma. Neither is the crucifixion a modern alteration to God's original plan for man.

The Predetermined Plan of God

To the contrary, God's mighty acts in salvation follow an ancient script that He decreed before the world began. His saving purposes carry out His predetermined plan designed from long ages ago. His rescuing works originated in eternity past. Redemption was sovereignly conceived before time began. The gospel is rooted and grounded in God's predestination, that weighty truth which guarantees all God's saving work.

This towering truth should have a monumental effect on preaching. The pulpit has always stood strongest when it has expounded the grace of God in salvation in the strongest terms. Without this immutable undergirding, sermons inevitably drift into shallow waters. Apart from this doctrine, preachers tend to aim at superficial concerns and offer temporal solutions.

But when preaching is anchored in God's supreme right to rule and reign, sinners are most soundly converted. Moreover, under this high teaching, believers are spiritually matured. If people's lives are to be well-established, the truth of predestination must be expounded in preaching.

A Needed Refocus

In this chapter, we will examine how, long before the human race sinned, God the Father predetermined the salvation of individual sinners. Paul has already made it clear that God powerfully calls to Himself (1 Corinthians 1:9,26) all whom He chooses to save (1:27-28). In eternity past, the Father foreknew the Son and chose to send Him into this world to secure salvation for those who would believe in Him (1 Peter 1:20). By His sovereign purpose, the Father commissioned the Holy Spirit to empower His preachers to proclaim the sinless life and saving death of the Son. And by His supreme power, the Spirit irresistibly calls every elect sinner to faith in Christ.

The preaching that God blesses is the preaching that magnifies the sovereign, saving purposes of all three persons of the Trinity. God the Father is Savior, God the Son is Savior, and God the Spirit is Savior. All three members of the Godhead work in perfect unity of purpose in saving the same chosen sinners.

Every preacher must be committed to preaching this full counsel of God. No biblical truth may be excluded. This includes the teaching that the Father predestined His sovereign grace for individual sinners in eternity past. But tragically, in the desire to avoid controversy, in order to escape difficult questions, many preachers avoid proclaiming these truths altogether. As though wanting to maintain the status quo, such men are reluctant to speak of God's predetermined grace in Christ. But silence is never an option in the preaching God blesses. To do so is to misrepresent the whole purpose of God. All truths established by God and recorded in His Word are to be embraced and proclaimed.

WE PREACH ETERNAL WISDOM

In 1 Corinthians 2:6-9, Paul addresses the subject of predestination. The apostle has already stated that God irresistibly calls to Himself all those whom He has chosen. He now focuses upon the divine wisdom by which God eternally predestined their salvation in Jesus Christ. This is true wisdom, which only the genius of God could design. In these verses, the key word is "wisdom," which the apostle Paul used 28 times in his epistles. Over half of these—a total of 15 times—appear in the first two chapters of 1 Corinthians alone. In addition, the adjective "wise" is used another ten times in 1 Corinthians 1–3. Clearly, Paul is calling our attention to the sheer genius of God in His eternal plan of salvation in Jesus Christ.

The Wisdom of the Cross

Throughout 1 Corinthians, Paul repeatedly emphasized the saving power of the cross. In the broader context, Paul addressed "the cross of Christ" (1:17), "the word of the cross" (1:18), "Christ crucified" (1:23), "Christ Jesus, who became to us wisdom from God, and righteousness and sanctification, and redemption" (1:30), and "Jesus Christ, and Him crucified" (2:2). For Paul, the cross was the greatest display of God's sovereign wisdom.

Moreover, the apostle Paul said that the cross is foundational for all Christian ministry (3:11). Likewise, the death of Christ is the very basis for believers living in moral purity

(5:7; 6:11,15,20). It is also the primary motive in Christian marriage (7:23), Christian liberty (8:11), and worship (11:23-26). In all Christian living, the cross is the primary message that needs to be embraced.

This divine wisdom was certainly preeminent in Paul's preaching. The apostle had nothing to say apart from this profound wisdom. The Lord Jesus must be preached as the all-saving, all-sanctifying Son of God for both sinners and saints alike. When Christ is proclaimed, we declare everything people need to hear. In short, Christ crucified was the epicenter of Paul's gospel message.

The Emptiness of Man's Wisdom

Paul stressed the divine wisdom of the cross because the Corinthians retained an infatuation with the human wisdom of the Greek culture. Before their conversion, the worldly philosophy of Athens shaped their worldview. When Paul came to Corinth, he preached the wisdom of the cross. By the power of the Spirit, the message of Christ crucified was received as true wisdom from God (1 Corinthians 1:30). Many people were converted. Yet they found it difficult to completely abandon human wisdom. Their love affair with secular reasoning still shaped what they believed and how they lived.

The believers in Corinth were so deeply entrenched in Greek thinking that they did not easily relinquish it. Though they embraced the apostle's teaching, they also maintained a strong grip on human wisdom. In a compromising move, they were attempting to consolidate cultural thinking with heavenly truth. Paul recognized this and was determined to correct their flawed thinking.

Divine wisdom and human thought cannot mix together. When secular philosophy was brought alongside divine theology, the result was a syncretistic approach that was devastating to their spiritual development. No wonder the Corinthian believers found themselves stunted in their growth in grace.

To Whom We Preach Wisdom

Paul rejected man's wisdom and taught an entirely different kind of wisdom—the wisdom of sovereign grace. He wrote, "We do speak wisdom" (1 Corinthians 2:6). By this emphatic statement, the apostle makes it clear that he was not opposed to all wisdom. To be sure, Paul *did* speak wisdom. Yet it was antithetical to human wisdom. He repudiated the wisdom of the world and instead proclaimed *true* wisdom from God.

To Those Who Are Mature

Divine wisdom, Paul said, is to be proclaimed "among those who are mature" (1 Corinthians 2:6). In this context, "mature" does not refer to spiritually advanced believers, as contrasted with immature believers. Rather, "mature" (Greek, *teleios*) refers to all genuine believers in Christ. This word can refer to one who has full membership in a group. That is the intended meaning here. Paul identifies all believers as those who are the "mature," who have a full inheritance of God's salvation in the cross.

Here, Paul urges that the death of Christ be preached to all believers. This message is not only for the lost, but also for the redeemed. The power of the cross is to be expounded to all people, whether unbelievers, spiritual babes, or those advanced in the faith. Christ crucified must be preached to every individual.

Always Needing This Wisdom

No one outgrows their spiritual need to hear the full-orbed message of the cross. No one ever reaches a point in their spiritual development where they no longer need to be taught the death of Christ. This fact is evidenced in the command that all believers are to repeatedly take part in the Lord's Supper.

The preaching of the cross is never out of place. The gospel is the power of God both for the salvation of unbelievers and for the sanctification of believers. God's wisdom in the cross is the greatest need for every Christian at every stage of spiritual development.

WISDOM FROM ABOVE

In no uncertain terms, Paul declared that divine wisdom does not come from the world. He said this wisdom is "not of this age nor of the rulers of this age, who are passing away"

(1 Corinthians 2:6). Paul told the Corinthian believers that such wisdom could not be found in the polluted Roman culture. It could not be heard from the Greek philosophers in Athens. Nor could it be discovered in the temples of pagan religions. Such wisdom comes exclusively from God.

Wisdom Not of This World

Neither does divine wisdom come, Paul wrote, from "the rulers of this age." It does not originate in the evil world system over which these earthly powers preside. These "rulers" oversee the same world order that violently crucified Jesus (1 Corinthians 2:8).

Such blind leaders, Paul stated, are "passing away." That is, they are perishing in their sins. So also are the world empires they represent. Without Christ, these world rulers are self-destructing.

By stark contrast, Paul reiterated, "we speak God's wisdom" (1 Corinthians 2:7). The apostle proclaimed a totally different kind of wisdom, which came from God alone. Absolutely nothing can be added to God's sheer brilliance in the cross of Jesus Christ.

In the same way that light is separate from darkness, divine wisdom is the polar opposite of human wisdom. Divine wisdom is eternal; man's wisdom is temporal. God's wisdom is divine; man's wisdom is demonic. God's wisdom is pure; man's wisdom is polluted by his fallen thinking.

Likewise, God's wisdom is cross-centered, while man's wisdom is cultured-centered. God's wisdom saves; man's wisdom damns. God's wisdom is heavenly; man's wisdom is earthly. The world perceives God's wisdom as foolish, but in actuality it is brilliant. And man's wisdom is thought to be brilliant, but it is entirely foolish.

Divine Wisdom in a Mystery

Regarding the preaching of the cross, Paul maintained this wisdom was "a mystery" that had been "hidden" until now (1 Corinthians 2:7)—it was a secret unknown to man. In the Bible, a "mystery" does not mean something puzzling or confusing. Rather, it is a truth known exclusively by God that He has kept to Himself. Mere human intelligence can never figure out a divine mystery—not until God chooses to reveal it by His own initiative.

This mystery is found in the gospel truth of Christ crucified. It is the divine solution that secures man's salvation. No matter how great a man's intellect, such a truth could never be discovered by his own insight. The only way this truth can be known is for God Himself to reveal it.

The cross is a truth that was partially hidden in the past but is now made known. In the fullness of time, the power of the cross was fully unveiled in the appearing of Christ. And today, preachers of the cross must declare this divine truth.

The coming of the Messiah had been prophesied in the Old Testament (Luke 24:27). It had been announced long ago that He would suffer, die, and be raised. This gospel truth was repeatedly emphasized in the apostles' preaching (Acts 2:25-28,30-31,34-35; 3:18,24; 7:52; 10:43).

But despite these Old Testament prophecies, the death of Christ was still regarded, relatively speaking, as a mystery in former times. Though the Old Testament pointed to Jesus, these messianic prophecies were still thinly veiled in types and shadows. Not until the appointed time was this mystery revealed.

PREDESTINED BEFORE THE WORLD

This divine wisdom in the cross is nothing new. The wisdom of Christ crucified was that "which God predestined before the ages" (1 Corinthians 2:7). The sin-bearing death of Christ was not a change in the divine plan. Neither was it an afterthought. Rather, it was the realization of God's eternal purpose in Christ. This mystery, fully revealed in the New Testament, was God's sovereign plan for saving sinners.

A Predetermined Destiny

The word "predestined" (Greek, *proorizo*) literally means "to mark out, appoint, or determine beforehand." The root of this verb comes into our English language as *horizon*. The idea is that the final destination of one's journey marked out on the horizon would come to pass.

The prefix *pre* means "before." The meaning is that the destination is already determined before the journey begins. "Predestined" designates one's final destiny on the distant horizon of eternity future. This destination was determined before the journey began.

In 1 Corinthians 2:7, God's predestination in salvation is grounded in the substitutionary death of Jesus Christ. The power to save chosen sinners was predestined by God. In eternity past, the Father foreordained the horrific death of His Son as the means to bring them to Himself.

Concerning Christ's crucifixion, God marked out that this event would come to pass. Before time began, the Father determined the path that His Son would take. Fixed in the eternal counsels of God was the death of Christ upon the cross. Moreover, God predestined at the cross the salvation of all His elect. This truth must be proclaimed again and again. This is the kind of preaching God blesses.

Preaching Predestination to All

On the day of Pentecost, Peter declared the predestining will of God in the death of Christ. This Spirit-empowered preacher thundered that Jesus was "delivered over by the predetermined plan and foreknowledge of God" (Acts 2:23). Emphatically, Peter announced that the cross was not an accident, but foreordained by God. Though the crucifixion was carried out by godless men, the death of Christ was the eternal sovereign will of God.

God's supreme right to rule in salvation was proclaimed by the early church. In the face of strong persecution, the first preachers delivered a yet stronger message. They announced the unalterable sovereignty of God concerning the death of His Son to save His people from their sins.

When Peter and John were imprisoned for preaching Jesus Christ and later released, their companions acknowledged that the death of Christ was according to God's sovereign purposes: "For truly in this city there were gathered together against Your holy servant Jesus, whom You anointed, both Herod and Pontius Pilate, along with the Gentiles and the peoples of Israel, to do whatever Your hand and Your purpose predestined to occur" (Acts 4:27-28).

This bold confession reveals the kind of lofty preaching these first believers had been hearing. The fact that they declared the predestining purposes of God in the death of Jesus Christ demonstrates the level of teaching they had received and the high view of divine sovereignty they had.

Such preaching on predestination is desperately needed today. What strength believers receive when they sit under strong affirmations of God's unalterable eternal plans with regard to human events and the salvation of sinners.

Guaranteed for Glory

Paul asserted that this divine wisdom is "to our glory" (1 Corinthians 2:7). In other words, the cross is the means by which God brings sinners to glory. This verse stretches from eternity past ("predestined") to eternity future ("glory"). Not only was the death of Christ predestined, but so also was the salvation of individual sinners predetermined to future glory.

In the sovereignly appointed death of Christ, the final glorification of all saints is irrevocably guaranteed. God's wisdom in the cross makes certain that everyone for whom Christ died will share in the future glory of heaven forever (John 10:11,14,16,26-30).

The kind of preaching that God blesses magnifies this sovereign grace. God looks favorably upon the pulpit that boldly declares His unalterable eternal purposes in the cross. He bestows power to the preacher who proclaims His supreme right in predestination. Such preaching acknowledges that He bestows His grace on whomever He pleases (Romans 9:15-18). This is the message that should sound forth from every pulpit today. Such high truth magnifies God and humbles man, crushes pride and promotes praise, lowers the creature and elevates the Creator. Such preaching declares the unrivaled, unhindered authority of God over all.

A LIFE WITHOUT WISDOM

Paul extended this argument as he elaborated on the spiritual blindness of the world rulers in crucifying Jesus. They failed to comprehend God's wisdom in the cross. The apostle described God's wisdom as that "which none of the rulers of this age has understood; for if they had understood it they would not have crucified the Lord of glory" (1 Corinthians 2:8). Those who crucified the Lord Jesus Christ did not understand the nature of God's sovereign wisdom.

God's saving purposes in Christ were veiled from the eyes of the Jewish and Roman leaders. Otherwise, they would not have carried out His perfect plan. In ignorance, they put Christ to death. But by God's eternal decree, it *had* to be so.

Blinded by the Light

Little did the Jewish and Roman leaders who crucified Jesus realize that they were actually carrying out God's predestined will. They were not in control of what took place; God was. These evil men thought they were killing a mere messianic pretender. They presumed they were putting to death a counterfeit christ. But in their ignorance, they crucified the Lord of glory.

To a large crowd in Jerusalem, Peter declared, "Brethren, I know that you acted in ignorance, just as your rulers did also" (Acts 3:17). These leaders failed to recognize Jesus as the Lord of glory. They were blind to the divine grandeur of Christ's perfect being. As fully God, Jesus possessed radiant splendor and dazzling glory. But they could not see it. The foolishness of the world is summed up in their execution of the all-glorious Lord of heaven and earth.

No man could have ever invented this plan of salvation by which God would send His only Son to die in the place of hell-bound sinners. No one could have conceived the arrangement by which Christ would shed His blood to propitiate the righteous anger of God toward the lost. No person could have designed this scheme by which Jesus would reconcile holy God to sinful man.

Furthermore, no one could have dreamed that Jesus would die in the place of sinners, be taken down from the cross, be buried in a borrowed tomb, and be raised on the third day—but *God* did.

Only God Himself could have designed this sovereign plan by which the risen Lord would ascend to the right hand of God the Father to be the Savior of all who will call upon Him. Only God could have purposed that all those who believe in Christ would be exalted in glory.

Hidden from Human Reason

Paul noted that the prophet Isaiah foretold of this stunningly brilliant plan of salvation. The apostle said, "Just as it is written, 'Things which eye has not seen and ear has not heard, and which have not entered the heart of man, all that God has prepared for those who love Him'" (1 Corinthians 2:9). Though this prophecy does not specifically identify this unseen reality, the context makes it clear that it refers to God's wisdom in the cross.

Specifically, Paul cited Isaiah to point out that the gospel cannot be learned by empirical observation ("eye has not seen"). This saving message is not passed down orally by tradition from one generation to the next ("ear has not heard"). The human heart cannot conceive such wisdom ("have not entered the heart of man"). God's wisdom is not discerned by intuitive insight. The divine wisdom in the cross is beyond mere natural thinking, beyond mere human comprehension.

Paul identifies the wisdom of the cross as "all that God has prepared for those who love Him" (1 Corinthians 2:9).

God prepared it beforehand in eternity past for all who would come to Him in Christ. Only God Himself can reveal this wisdom to man, and He does so by the divine revelation of the Scripture and the divine illumination of the Spirit.

A SACRED TRUST

This lofty message of God's predestining purposes in the cross has been entrusted to all whom He has called to preach His Word. The high honor of declaring the unimaginable wisdom of God in the cross has been committed to such privileged men. This profound truth is far beyond the intelligence of any man to conceive. It is the sacred word entrusted to those divinely commissioned to preach.

These preachers are to make known what no human mind could ever understand apart from divine revelation. In light of this, no greater privilege could ever be afforded than making known this crucified Christ.

Because God is sovereign in the salvation of sinners, the preacher is simply required to be faithful in presenting biblical truth. He must then leave the results with God. When the gospel reaches the elect, God will summon them to faith in Christ. Therefore, the preacher does not need to manipulate the listener. He does not need to resort to gimmicks that trivialize the message. Neither does he need to appeal to cohesive techniques that produce false results. He merely needs to present the truth in the power of the Spirit, trusting God for the response.

This is not to say that the preacher should not be passionate or persuasive in presenting the truth. Neither does it mean he should not preach with a sense of dire urgency. But it does mean that he will not attempt to induce a response in those to whom he brings the Word. Further, he must not distort the message in order to force the conversion of his listeners. Nor may he tamper with the work of the Spirit. To the contrary, the preacher God blesses preaches the Word with the full force of convictions, but leaves the results with the sovereignty of God.

THE UNCHANGING SUBJECT

Whether you stand in a pulpit or serve in a prison, whether you take the gospel into a hospital or onto a college campus, the heart of your witness must be the cross of Jesus Christ. Wherever you go, to whomever you speak, you must preach Jesus Christ crucified for sinners. No matter who your audience is, your message remains the same. You are to preach the predetermined purpose of God in the substitutionary death of Christ.

Every preacher must preach Christ crucified in order to fulfill his sacred calling. It does not matter what else he does—if he does not preach Christ crucified, he is not true to the divine mandate assigned to him.

Charles Spurgeon certainly understood this mandate. He firmly believed that he had received marching orders from his Master to stand at the foot of the cross and remain there until He returned. As long as he lived, he was to tell this simple story of Christ crucified to a perishing world. Spurgeon declared:

> I received some years ago orders from my Master to stand at the foot of the cross until He came. He has not come yet, but I mean to stand there till He does. If I should disobey His orders and leave those simple truths which have been the means of the conversion of souls, I know not how I could expect His blessing. Here, then, I stand at the foot of cross and tell out the old, old story, stale though it sound to itching ears, and worn threadbare as critics may deem it. It is of Christ I love to speak—of Christ who loved, and lived, and died, the substitute for sinners, the just for the unjust, that He might bring us to God.[25]

Every preacher has received these same marching orders. Where Spurgeon stood at the foot of the cross, so we must stand. With our gaze fixed upon His glory above, we must preach this saving grace until Jesus returns. May we be found faithful in this call to proclaim the message of the sovereign wisdom of God in the cross of Jesus Christ. And when He returns, may we be found faithfully standing at the foot of the cross.

6
Marching Orders

The Parade of Faithful Preachers

As has been stated throughout this book, there is a kind of preaching that God blesses. Those pulpits that follow the pattern established by Paul in 1 Corinthians 2:1-9 are well-positioned to know this divine favor. This is the approach to preaching to which every expositor must be committed. Every herald of truth bears personal responsibility to emulate the apostolic model set forth by Paul in this important passage.

No preacher is free to vary his doctrine from what Paul taught. Every man must preach only those truths asserted in the Bible. At the same time, neither may anyone stand in a pulpit and alter his delivery from what is exemplified by the apostle. The Scripture teaches *what* we are to preach and *how* we are to preach it. The Bible establishes both the *message* and the *manner* in which God's truth is to be proclaimed. The fact is, it matters to God how His Word is preached.

In this pointed text, Paul has laid out a timeless model for every preacher to follow. Regardless of where or to whom one ministers, these principles transcend centuries, continents, and cultures. Here, the apostle recorded the essential core of what he preached and how he presented it. For this reason, we must closely adhere to the instruction in these verses.

TWO ASPECTS OF PROCLAMATION

The Science of Exposition

In order to rightly understand expository preaching, one must recognize that this approach to the pulpit is both a science and art. Such preaching is a science in that there are unalterable laws which govern its success. These principles include the fixed laws of interpretation, known as hermeneutics, or the science of interpretation.

This disciplined approach involves a careful investigation of the text that considers word studies, grammar, syntax, verb tenses, historical background, geography, culture, and more. There are unbreakable tenets associated with each of these areas of study that must be kept in order to rightly interpret what God means by what He says. All proper interpretation of the biblical text must follow these fixed rules.

If these basic laws of hermeneutics are broken, the sermon will, tragically, misrepresent the Scripture and fail to honor God. Any message that mishandles Scripture, distorting its true meaning, is devoid of God's blessing. Any forced imposition upon the text—that is, a contrived meaning—will fail to accurately communicate what God is saying. Such a loose approach reads into the text what God never said.

The Bible is written to communicate objective truth in definite words that have precise meanings. Understanding the meaning of the text requires objective principles of interpretation so that the preacher might rightly understand what God is saying.

The preaching that God blesses must faithfully represent a proper understanding of any passage of Scripture. God will bless only that which rightly interprets the true meaning of the text.

The Art of Preaching

At the same time, biblical exposition is also an art. This is to say, preaching allows for some creativity and individuality from one minister to the next. This variance allows, and even demands, for one's unique personality to come through the sermon. Moreover, this diversity calls for a difference between one sermon and another, even by the same preacher. Otherwise, every sermon from the same text should be word-for-word the same.

Among different preachers, there should never be a difference in *interpretation* of the biblical text. To be sure, there is only one proper interpretation of a passage. Rather, any difference in sermons must lie in the packaging and presentation. While the substance of each sermon should be essentially the same, there is room for specific truths to be presented and applied in a variety of ways.

Succinctly stated, no two preachers are the same. Neither are any two congregations to which their sermons are presented. Nor are any two situations the same. Thus, sermons will always differ, but never in their doctrine—only in their emphasis and delivery.

Consequently, preaching will differ as each preacher differs. Each man has his own unique personality, temperament, maturity, age, experience, and giftedness. No two expositors are wired quite the same. Nor are any two preachers at the same place in their spiritual life. This variance allows for, even necessitates, differences from one sermon to the next, just as one preacher differs from the next.

Regarding congregations, different groups of listeners are at different places in their spiritual walk with the Lord. They are comprised of people at different levels of spiritual maturity, of different ages, with different amounts of exposure to the truth, and different backgrounds. Thus, an expositor must learn to adapt his sermons accordingly.

How a preacher addresses one group may differ from how he addresses the next. How he speaks to the same congregation over a period of many years may differ as time goes by. These differences will depend upon the spiritual maturity of a group at any particular time. This is the art of expository preaching—taking into consideration different approaches to the application, different kinds of illustrations, different approaches to the introduction, different tones to the delivery, and different types of conclusions. The expositor must be keenly aware of all these factors as he crafts his sermon for those to whom he speaks.

When it comes to the science and the art of preaching, wise is the man who acknowledges these two aspects of proclamation and embraces both.

NEEDED: TRINITARIAN PREACHING

The preaching that God blesses must be distinctly Trinitarian. It is preaching in which all three persons of the Godhead are actively involved. Father, Son, and Holy Spirit must be seen in their proper Trinitarian roles.

Jesus Christ: The Preeminent Subject in Preaching

First, the preeminent subject of preaching must be the person and work of Jesus Christ. As plainly stated by Paul, "We preach Christ crucified" (1 Corinthians 1:23). The mandate for any minister could not be clearer. The focal point of all preaching must be Jesus Christ in His saving death.

Such Christ-centered preaching is constantly exalting Him and pointing its listeners to Him. The sum and substance of God-favored preaching is rooted in the faithful proclamation of the second person of the Godhead, Jesus Christ. In the simplest terms possible, Paul announces,

"We proclaim Him" (Colossians 1:28). Christ must be the heart and soul of all we proclaim.

Jesus did this in His own teaching. He said, "You search the Scriptures because you think that in them you have eternal life; it is these that testify about Me" (John 5:39). Here, Jesus said that He is the One to whom the body of Scripture bears supreme witness. Put another way, the main theme of Scripture is Jesus Christ. The entire Bible points to Him. Following His resurrection, He addressed two disciples on the road to Emmaus and "explained to them the things concerning Himself in all the Scriptures" (Luke 24:27). He explained how the prophecies about the Messiah looked forward to Himself.

Throughout the Old and New Testaments, there is only one way of salvation, and it is through Jesus Christ. Saints in the Old Testament were saved by looking ahead to Christ, just as believers in the New Testament are saved by looking back at His death and resurrection. Salvation by grace alone, through faith alone, in Christ alone, is the unifying theme of Scripture. To preach the Bible, therefore, necessitates that one preach Christ.

Is Christ central in your preaching? Does He have unrivaled preeminence in all that you teach and declare? Is He the glorious theme in all your pulpit ministry? To be sure, the kind of preaching God blesses is riveted upon Christ crucified.

The Holy Spirit: The Supernatural Power in Preaching

Second, all preaching must be done in the power of the Holy Spirit. No one can effectively proclaim the Lord Jesus in his own strength. The saving power is in the divine message and not the messenger. Nevertheless, he must have God's power in order to deliver God's truths. The preacher will know divine blessing upon his ministry as long as his proclamation is by the fullness of the Holy Spirit.

The third member of the Godhead delights in magnifying Christ. "The Spirit of truth" (John 14:17; 15:26; 16:13) must illumine the preacher's mind to understand the truths concerning Christ in the Scriptures. The Spirit must enflame his heart, deepen his convictions, and enlarge his compassion, yet with boldness, as he preaches Christ (Acts 4:8; 1 Thessalonians 1:5). Only the omnipotent Spirit can do this in His servants.

Preaching that knows God's favor must be empowered by His Spirit. The preacher must be filled with the Spirit if he is to speak God's Word to others (Ephesians 5:18-19). He must not quench the Spirit by relying simply on his giftedness apart from a dependence upon God's Spirit.

Do you preach with a conscious awareness of your need for the Spirit's enablement? Do you know the empowering of the Spirit's grace? Do you pray for His divine ministry in your preaching? Are you aware that when you stand in the pulpit, there must be two who stand before an open Bible? The kind of preaching God blesses is Spirit-anointed preaching.

The Father: The Predetermined Wisdom in Preaching

Third, true preaching must proclaim the gospel message that was foreordained by God before the foundation of the world. If preaching is to be divinely favored, it must declare His sovereign will in salvation.

Tragically, many preachers, in their attempt to be contemporary, neglect teaching the full counsel of God. They seek to present to gospel in a manner that is easy to hear, but in so doing, they withhold certain difficult truths that people find hard to accept. There must be a full disclosure of the truth. Nothing should be held back. If God has put a truth in His Word, then it must be proclaimed. The truth of divine sovereignty in salvation is no exception.

The preaching that God blesses declares the predetermined plan of redemption that He authored in eternity past. We must preach the truth of the sovereign election of God in His foreordaining grace. We must proclaim that God has chosen a people for Himself (Ephesians 1:4-5). Moreover, He has chosen Christ to be their Savior (1 Peter 1:20). The eternal gospel must be faithfully preached to every generation.

Do you preach the sovereign authority of God in salvation? Do you magnify His eternal purposes in saving sinners?

Do you remain steadfast in proclaiming the gospel message in its entirety to the lost and perishing of this world?

A LONG LINE OF FAITHFUL MEN

Down through the centuries, there has been a long line of faithful preachers who have followed this apostolic pattern in preaching. These stalwarts of the faith have heroically upheld the eternal message of Christ and Him crucified in their appointed hour of human history. They served as devoted stewards of the mysteries of Christ, dedicated messengers of the gospel who proclaimed the one central theme of all Scripture—namely, the Lord Jesus Christ. They were deeply convinced that as long as they were on this earth, their primary purpose was to proclaim the message of the cross.

They have remained reliable mouthpieces for God. They have preached the message which He foreordained before time began. They have preached His Word without compromising its truths. And they have carried out their preaching in the power of the Holy Spirit.

This is the kind of preaching God blesses.

What about you? Will you be numbered among this faithful remnant? Will you be among the few who commit to preaching the glories of Christ? Will you be among history's handful who will proclaim Him in the power of the Holy Spirit? Will you be among those who remain true to the eternal message of God?

TWO INSTRUMENTS IN GOD'S HAND

Two preachers who stand out in church history are the nineteenth-century Scottish preachers Andrew Bonar and Robert Murray M'Cheyne. Andrew was the younger brother of the famous hymn writer Horatius Bonar, and M'Cheyne became an eminent Scottish preacher. Bonar and M'Cheyne were the same age and attended the same elementary school in Edinburgh. The two were close friends.

At the age of 18, M'Cheyne was converted to Christ at the death of his eldest brother, David. Robert said it was then that he began to seek "a Brother who cannot die."[26] He then turned to Jesus Christ in faith and entered into the kingdom of God.

In short time, M'Cheyne entered the ministry and became a mighty preacher of the gospel. He was a principal instrument in bringing about the Kilsyth Revival (1838–1839) in Scotland. This mighty movement of God was marked by the powerful preaching of the cross by both M'Cheyne and Bonar.

This, in turn, spurred Bonar and M'Cheyne to reach the world together for Christ. Concerned for the salvation of the Jewish people, Bonar and M'Cheyne traveled to Palestine in 1839, not as tourists, but to do the demanding work of preaching the gospel to unconverted Jews.

M'Cheyne: Dying at Age 29

While in the Promised Land, M'Cheyne and Bonar preached Christ. This was one of the most difficult places in the world to do the work of evangelism. After ministering there for a while they returned to Scotland, where they continued to serve the Lord with unusual abandonment and extraordinary devotion. In their service for the Lord, these two men pushed themselves to the extreme.

But the rigorous demands of young Robert's ministry endeavors were more than his physical body could bear. This energetic soul burned himself out for Christ, and he died at the tender age of 29.

After M'Cheyne died, his close friend, Andrew, compiled his diary and journal as *Memoir and Remains of Rev. Robert Murray M'Cheyne* (1862). Andrew also wrote a biography of M'Cheyne so that the world would know of Robert's devotion for Christ. This book would become a Christian devotional classic, inspiring others to go to the mission field.

Bonar: Preaching Until Age 82

Unlike his friend M'Cheyne, Bonar would live for more than another half-century. He remained in pastoral ministry for 54 years. When Bonar died, he was still pastoring in Glasgow, Scotland, at 82 years old.

Before he died, Bonar reflected, "*Why* would my best friend Robert Murray M'Cheyne die at age twenty-nine while I lived so long? *Why* would I be allowed to live into my eighties? *Why* am I spared so long?"[27]

To his mind came this answer: "One thing I know. It must be that I may preach Christ and Him crucified whenever and wherever it is in my power."[28] Bonar believed that he had been given a long life for this chief reason: that he might preach Christ and Him crucified.

FAITHFUL TO THE END

Even so, this is the purpose that every preacher is given whatever years he has to live. All who are messengers of grace must plainly understand that *this* is our primary reason for being alive. As long as we draw breath, we must proclaim Christ and Him crucified.

Why are you on this earth? Why has God allowed you to live as long as you have? Why is there still blood coursing through your veins? Why is there still strength in your body? Surely the answer must be that as long as you find yourself here upon this earth, it is so that you may boldly proclaim the glorious news of Jesus Christ and Him crucified.

This is why we, as heralds of the gospel, are allowed to remain alive. It is so that we may sound forth God's message to a lost and dying world. This is the highest purpose we can ever attain to.

And God's favor will be upon our preaching so long as we are faithful to declare Christ and Him crucified. This, and this alone, is the kind of preaching that God blesses.

Let us, therefore, stand firm in our commitment to Trinitarian preaching. Let us renounce the message and methodologies of this fallen world that would seek to consign Christ to the periphery in preaching. Let us be steadfast in our devotion to uphold Christ and Him crucified in our every proclamation from the pulpit.

This is the preaching God blesses.

Notes

1. Michael Horton, *Christless Christianity* (Grand Rapids: Baker Books, 2008), 16-17.

2. Horton, *Christless Christianity*, 18.

3. C.H. Spurgeon, as cited by Lewis A. Drummond, *Spurgeon: Prince of Preachers* (Grand Rapids: Kregel, 1992), 223.

4. C.H. Spurgeon, *The Metropolitan Tabernacle Pulpit, Vol. XIV* (Pasadena, TX: Pilgrim Publications, 1970, 1976, 1982), 467.

5. The source of this quote popularly attributed to Lloyd-Jones is unknown.

6. Boice, *Whatever Happened to the Gospel of Grace?*, 26.

7. Martin Luther, *Luther's Works,* vol. 51, ed. John W. Doberstein (Philadelphia: Fortress, 1959), 77.

8. Martin Luther as quoted in Roy B. Zuck, *The Speaker's Quote Book* (Grand Rapids: Kregel Academic, 1997), 308.

9. Rev. John Ker, *Lectures on the History of Preaching* (London: Hodder and Stoughton, 1888), 154-56.

10. Martin Luther, *The Cambridge Companion to Martin Luther*, ed. Donald K. McKim (Cambridge, UK: Cambridge University Press, 2003), 138.

11. Gustav Friedrich, "*kerygma*," ed. Gerhard Kittel, *Theological Dictionary of the New Testament* (Grand Rapids: Eerdmans, 1965), 3:687-88.

12. Friedrich, "*kerygma*," ed. Kittel, *Theological Dictionary of the New Testament*, 3:687-88.

13. C.H. Spurgeon, *The Metropolitan Tabernacle Pulpit, Vol. VII*, 169.

14. C.H. Spurgeon, *Lectures to My Students* (Pasadena, TX: Pilgrim Publications, 1977), 82.

15. D. Martyn Lloyd-Jones, *Preaching & Preachers* (Grand Rapids: Zondervan, 1971), 95.

16. Lloyd-Jones, *Preaching & Preachers*, 305.

17. Lloyd-Jones, *Preaching & Preachers*, 324.

18. Lloyd-Jones, *Preaching & Preachers*, 324.

19. C.H. Spurgeon, *Lectures to My Students, Second Series* (London: Passmore and Alabaster, 1881), 91.

20. John Murray, *Collected Writings of John Murray, Vol. 3* (Edinburgh: Banner of Truth, 1982), 72.

21. R.C. Sproul, *The Preacher and Preaching*, ed. Samuel T. Logan, Jr. (Phillipsburg, NJ: P & R Publishing, 1986), 113.

22. Richard Baxter, *The Reformed Pastor* (Carlisle, PA: The Banner of Truth Trust, 1656, 1829, 1862, 1974, 1979), 148.

23. Baxter, *The Reformed Pastor*.

24. Adrian Rogers, *The Power of His Presence* (Wheaton, IL: Crossway, 1995), 56.

25. C.H. Spurgeon as cited in Drummond, *Spurgeon*, 289.

26. Andrew Bonar, *The Memoirs & Remains of Robert Murray M'Cheyne* (Edinburgh, Scotland: The Banner of Truth Trust, 2004), 11.

27. Andrew Bonar, *Diary & Life* (Edinburgh, Scotland: The Banner of Truth Trust, 1984), 184.

28. Bonar, *Diary & Life,* 525.